Woodstock Public Library

W9-ACZ-276

Love Your Enemies

How Decent People Can Save America from the Culture of Contempt

Arthur C. Brooks

An Imprint of HarperCollinsPublishers

LOVE YOUR ENEMIES. Copyright © 2019 by the American Enterprise Institute. All rights reserved. Printed in the United States of America. No part of this book may be used or reproduced in any manner whatsoever without written permission except in the case of brief quotations embodied in critical articles and reviews. For information, address HarperCollins Publishers, 195 Broadway, New York, NY 10007.

HarperCollins books may be purchased for educational, business, or sales promotional use. For information, please e-mail the Special Markets Department at SPsales@harpercollins.com.

FIRST HARPERLUXE EDITION

ISBN: 978-0-06-288802-0

HarperLuxe™ is a trademark of HarperCollins Publishers.

Library of Congress Cataloging-in-Publication Data is available upon request.

20 21 22 23 ID/LSC 10 9 8 7 6 5

To the memory of
Father Arne Panula

We are not enemies, but friends. We must not be enemies. Though passion may have strained, it must not break our bonds of affection. The mystic chords of memory, stretching from every battlefield and patriot grave to every living heart and hearthstone all over this broad land, will yet swell the chorus of the Union when again touched, as surely they will be, by the better angels of our nature.

—ABRAHAM LINCOLN, First Inaugural Address

Contents

Contents

Love Your Enemies

LOVE YOUR ENEMIES

Introduction
Are You Sick of Fighting Yet?

I confess without shame, I am tired & sick of war.
Its glory is all moonshine.

—GENERAL WILLIAM TECUMSEH SHERMAN, 1865

I live and work in Washington, DC, but I'm not a politics junkie. To me, politics is like the weather. It changes a lot, people drone on about it constantly, and "good" is totally subjective. I like winter, you like summer; you're a liberal, I'm a conservative. Furthermore, political opinions are like noses: No two are totally alike, but everyone has one. My nose is big, but its existence is utterly unremarkable—sort of like my political opinions.

My thing is *ideas*, especially *policy ideas*. While politics is like the weather, ideas are like the climate. Climate has a big impact on the weather, but it's not the same thing. Similarly, ideas affect politics, but they aren't the same.

When done right, policy analysis, like climate science, favors nerds with PhDs. And that's me. I have a PhD in policy analysis; for my doctorate I studied applied microeconomics and mathematical modeling. I taught policy at a university for ten years, before becoming the president of a public policy think tank in Washington, DC, a job I've held for a decade. (Before graduate school, I spent twelve years making my living as a musician, but not the cool kind. I played the French horn in a symphony orchestra. So yeah—*nerd-o-rama*.)

Having a little distance from politics has made it so that even in the heart of DC, I don't usually take political battles too seriously. In the 2012 presidential election season, my wife and I had a bumper sticker custom-made for the Volvo—VEGANS FOR ROMNEY—just to see the reaction of other DC drivers.

However, even a climate scientist has to think about the weather when a hurricane comes ashore, and that's what's happening today. Political differences are ripping our country apart, rendering my big, fancy policy ideas largely superfluous. Political scientists find that our nation is more polarized than it has been at any time since the Civil War. This is especially true among partisan elites—leaders who, instead of bringing us together, depict our differences in unbridgeable, apocalyptic terms.[1]

As much as we'd like to, we can't joke the problem away. The only truly funny thing I've seen in our miserable political culture was a bumper sticker in the run-up to November 2016 that read GIANT METEOR 2016, suggesting that a humanity-ending catastrophe would be better than the election's political choices. As my daughter would say, "That's dark, man."

I remember when I first recognized the force of this hurricane, two and a half years before the 2016 election. I was speaking to a large group of conservative activists in New Hampshire. Public speeches are a big part of what I do for a living, and I address audiences all across the political spectrum. It is the thing I most enjoy about my work. I love meeting people and sharing ideas. It never gets old. This particular audience was an ideological home-field crowd for me, too, because the event was focused on the moral virtues of free enterprise. While I'm not a member of either political party, free enterprise is something I deeply believe in.

I was the only nonpolitician on the schedule, and arriving a little early, I listened to a few of the other speakers before I went on. One after another told the audience that they were right and the opposing political side was wrong. By the time I went onstage, the crowd was pretty fired up. My speech was about how people naturally perceive conservatives and liberals in America today. I made the point that liberals are widely considered to be compassionate and empathetic, and that conservatives should work to earn this reputation as well.

After the speech, a woman in the audience came up to me, and she was clearly none too happy with my comments. I thought she was going to criticize my assertion that conservatives are not thought to be as compassionate as liberals. Instead, she told me that I was being too nice to liberals. "They are not compassionate and empathetic," she said. "They are stupid and evil." She argued that as a public figure, I was obliged to say so plainly because "*It's the truth.*"

At that moment, my thoughts went to . . . Seattle. That's where I grew up. While my own politics tend more center-right, Seattle is arguably the most politically liberal place in the United States. My father was a college professor; my mother was an artist. Professors and artists in Seattle . . . what do *you* think their politics were?

So when that woman in New Hampshire said that liberals are stupid and evil, she wasn't talking about me, but she *was* talking about my family. Without meaning to, she was effectively presenting me with a choice: my loved ones or my ideology. Either I admit that those with whom I disagree politically—including people I love— are stupid and evil, or I renounce my ideas and my credibility as a public figure. Love or ideology: choose.

Have you been subjected to a similar choice? Have you been told by a newspaper pundit, politician, college professor, or television host that your friends, family, and neighbors on the other side are knaves and fools, implying that if you have any integrity, you must stand up to them or leave them behind? That people with a different perspective hate our country and must be completely destroyed? That if you're not outraged, you're not paying attention? That kindness to your ideological foes is tantamount to weakness?

Whether your politics are on the left, right, or center, most likely you have, and it might just be affecting your life. For example, a January 2017 Reuters/Ipsos poll found that one in six Americans had *stopped talking to a family member or close friend* because of the 2016 election.[2] A far bigger share of the population has sorted social life along ideological lines over the past few years, by avoiding the places where people disagree with them, curating their news and social media to weed out opposing viewpoints, and seeking out the spaces—from college campuses to workplaces—where they find the most ideological compatriots.

We are being driven apart, which is the last thing we need in what is a fragile moment for our country. America isn't in the midst of an economic collapse as we were in 2008, but we've faced major challenges in the past decade—economically, socially, and geopolitically. Ten years after the Great Recession, millions feel traumatized by political shifts, cultural change, and the uncertainties of a modern, globalized world.

This is reflected in the deep pessimism felt throughout the country even in the face of economic improvement. In a dramatically strengthening economy, more than four in ten Americans say they think the nation's best years are behind us.[3] Unemployment is the lowest it's been in decades, and yet three-quarters of Americans still say that either "The middle class does not feel needed or useful in what they are doing and the work that they do," or "The middle class feels value in what they are doing . . . but are not valued by the nation's elites and institutions."[4]

We need national healing every bit as much as economic growth. But what are we getting instead from many of our leaders in media, politics, entertainment, and academia? Across the political spectrum, people in positions of power and influence are setting us against one another. They tell us our neighbors who disagree with us politically are ruining our country. That ideological differences aren't a matter of differing opinions but reflect moral turpitude. That our side must utterly vanquish the other, even if it leaves our neighbors without a voice.

In the very moment in which America most needs to come together as a nation—in the early decades of what, for the good of the world, *should* be a new American century—we are being torn apart, thoughtlessly and needlessly. We are living in a culture of contempt.

We need to fight back. But how?

"We were ready to fight."

On September 16, 2017, Hawk Newsome and a group of protesters from Black Lives Matter of Greater New York arrived on the National Mall in Washington, DC, to confront a group of Trump supporters gathered for what they called the "Mother of All Rallies." A community activist from the South Bronx, Hawk had recently been on the front lines in Charlottesville, Virginia, protesting a rally by white nationalists that had made headlines all over the country. He was still nursing a wound from that confrontation, where he had been hit in the face with a rock.

When Hawk and his team arrived on the Mall, he

braced for another confrontation, and maybe more in-
juries. He figured the pro-Trump marchers were not
much different from the white supremacists he had
faced in Charlottesville. Hawk was filled with disdain
for them. The marchers appeared to reciprocate his feelings, yelling, "USA! USA! You don't like it, get out!"
and, "Ignore them! They don't exist!" The two sides
traded insults, and the situation became more combustible by the second. Onlookers immediately pulled out
their iPhones and became ersatz videographers, ready to
capture the clash and post on social media. It was clear
that yet another one of those ugly confrontations we have
all come to dread was about to unfold.

But then, just as the insults seemed ready to give
way to blows, something wholly unexpected happened.
Tommy Hodges, the organizer of the pro-Trump rally,
invited Hawk Newsome onto his stage. "We're going to
give you two minutes of our platform to put your message out," Tommy told Hawk. "Whether they disagree
or agree with your message is irrelevant. It's the fact that
you have the right to have the message."

Hawk was ready to fight, not give a speech, but he
accepted nonetheless. As he took the microphone in
his hand, he thought back to a moment in Charlottesville when he was about to pick up a rock and throw it.
"This little old white lady, I don't know where she came

from, but she said, 'Your mouth is your most powerful weapon. You don't need anything but that.'" Now Hawk had a chance to use it. A committed Christian, he said a prayer, and as he did, he heard a voice in his heart telling him, *Let them know who you are.* He took a deep breath and addressed the hostile crowd with passion and total sincerity.

"My name is Hawk Newsome. I am the president of Black Lives Matter New York. I am an American."

He had the crowd's attention, and he continued. "And the beauty of America is that when you see something broken in your country, you can mobilize to fix it," he said.

To his utter surprise, the crowd burst into applause. Emboldened, he said, "So you ask why there's a Black Lives Matter? Because you can watch a black man die and be choked to death on television and nothing happened. We need to address that."

"That was a criminal," someone yelled, as boos started emanating from the crowd.

Hawk pressed on. "We're not anti-cop."

"Yes you are!" someone yelled.

"We're anti–*bad* cop," Hawk countered. "We say if a cop is bad he needs to get fired like a bad plumber, like a bad lawyer, like a bad . . . politician."

At this, the crowd began cheering again. These days,

there's nothing political ralliers hate more than bad politicians.

"I said that I am an American. Secondly, I am a Christian," Hawk said, once again connecting with his audience. "We don't want handouts. We don't want anything that's yours. We want our God-given right to freedom, liberty, and the pursuit of happiness."

The crowd erupted in cheers.

Then someone shouted, "All lives matter!"

"You're right, my brother, you're right. You are so right," Hawk said. "All lives matter, right? But when a black life is lost, we get no justice. That is why we say black lives matter."

His two minutes up, he concluded his remarks by saying, "Listen, I want to leave you with this, and I'm gone. If we really want to make America great, we do it together!"

The crowd roared. They started chanting "USA! USA!" A lady standing in the front row reached up and handed Hawk an American flag. He held it up and waved it. More cheers. As he stepped off the stage, to his shock and amazement, many of the Trump supporters came up and embraced him. Earlier, when he first arrived on the Mall, he had cut his hand with a knife while opening a box of signs. He had wrapped it in a bandanna, but now it was bleeding through. The leader of a four-thousand-man militia saw that Hawk was hurt and took him aside to treat his wound. "He's treating my finger," Hawk says, "and the militia guy goes, 'You know, I thought I understood before, but I get it now. You're all right, brother.' We slapped hands." They have kept in touch since the rally. "We're still friends on Facebook," Hawk says.

Then a man named Kenny Johnson, one of the leaders of a group called Bikers for Trump, approached Hawk. "He's like a *Sons of Anarchy* type," Hawk recalls. "He said, 'Your speech was amazing. I'd be honored if you met my son.' So we walked over to see his son, who was playing with his toys under a tree. A little blond-haired kid named Jacob." Johnson asked Hawk to pick the boy up so they could take a picture together. "That touched me," Hawk says.

After meeting Hawk, Johnson told *Vice News*, "I feel what he said came from his heart when he got on the stage. I probably agree with 90 percent of what he said. I listened to him with much love, respect, and honor, and I got that back, so as far as I'm concerned he's my brother now."[5]

Brotherhood was evidently breaking out all over the National Mall that day. "It was euphoric," Hawk says. "It kind of restored my faith in some of those people. Because when I spoke truths, they agreed. I feel like we made progress . . . without either side yielding." He had arrived expecting conflict. Instead, he says, "I went from being their enemy to someone they want to take pictures with their children."

Hawk told me the experience changed him. After returning to New York, he says, "I wrestled with myself for a few months." Finally, he made a decision. "I decided I'd rather go with love. I'm not out to blast people anymore. I'm not out to argue, to fight. I'm there to make people understand, to make people come together. I'm here for progress."

He got a lot of blowback from some in his own activist community, who did not like his sharing a stage with the pro-Trump demonstrators. Some people called him a "KKK-loving Trump supporter." One activist declared Hawk had "committed treason." He is undeterred by the criticism. "This divide that's keeping us from speaking to one another, from understanding one another, we can overcome it," he says, but "we don't get there by screaming at each other all the time. We get there by building bridges. So my language has changed. Because what happened on that stage was great. . . . It's a new day . . . there's a new way to do this."

Tommy Hodges agrees. After the rally, he gave an interview in which he explained why he had invited Hawk onto the stage. "We have so much political violence that's happening right now," he said. "I mean, every day you turn on the news, you turn on social media, all you see is people being attacked for their political views. It's absurd. . . . Political violence happens in Russia. It happens in Iran. It happens in North Korea. It's not supposed to happen here.

"It's time to bring everybody together, and get everybody to celebrate America together. . . . So if you are an American, no matter what your color, creed, demographic, political beliefs are, if you're an American, and you love this country, [you are welcome to] come out and celebrate with us," Hodges said. "We need to set a new standard. . . . It's time that people shake hands and agree to disagree. And if people can't do that, this country is going to fall apart."[6]

While national media mostly ignored what happened on the Mall that day, it became an underground viral sensation. Fifty-seven million people watched Hawk's speech on the Internet. Seemingly everyone who saw it, regardless of politics, sent the video on to friends and family with the same message: This is incredible! You have to see this!

That's how I first saw the video. When the Trump supporters started applauding, my heart swelled. I was so inspired by it that I wrote about the encounter in the *New York Times*, and became friends myself with Hawk

Newsome. Go online and watch the video yourself and listen to your own heart as you do. I'll make you a bet: If you're like most Americans, no matter what your politics, you won't be hoping that Hawk gets booed off that stage. You will be rooting for Hawk Newsome—and you will be rooting for the pro-Trump crowd to cheer for him.

You won't be alone. Just look at the comments section beneath the video:

> "Progress! It's happening and all the hate in the
>   world can't stop it!"
> "We need more of this. We should be able to
>   disagree on things, and still be respectful."
> "This is a truly beautiful video."
> "That brought tears to my eyes."
> "Wow, this is so powerful!! . . . Unity is what is
>   going to make the world a better place for all."

At the beginning of this introduction, I defined our national problem as a culture of contempt. What exactly is contempt?

Social scientists define contempt as anger mixed with disgust.[7] These two emotions form a toxic combination, like ammonia mixed with bleach. In the words of the nineteenth-century philosopher Arthur Schopenhauer, contempt is "the unsullied conviction of the worthlessness of another."[8] Deriving from the Latin word *contemptus*, meaning "scorn," contempt represents not merely an outburst following a moment of deep frustration with another but rather an enduring attitude of complete disdain.[9]

This description of contempt will sound familiar to many because contempt has become the leitmotif of modern political discourse. We saw this at the outset of the rally in Washington, DC. We see it on cable television and social media, and increasingly, we see it in person. But if our responses to the interaction between Tommy and Hawk tell us anything, it is that contempt isn't what we actually want. More important, our responses tell us that the choice between either political ideology or our friends and family, so often peddled by leaders today, is a *false choice*. A moment like this reveals that Americans have been manipulated and bullied into thinking that we have to choose between strong beliefs and close relationships. Deep down, we all know that the polarization we are experiencing in our politics today is toxic. We hate the fighting, the insults, the violence and disrespect.

Tommy and Hawk inadvertently showed the hunger of Americans for another way. I have seen for myself that this message of kindness in the face of contempt is one that resonates widely. The same year as the rally in Washington, I gave a speech at Harvard University's Kennedy School. Harvard posted a sixty-second video of the talk. Here's a transcript of that video, lightly edited for clarity:

We don't have an anger problem in American politics. We have a contempt problem. . . . If you listen to how people talk to each other in political life today, you notice it is with pure contempt.

When somebody around you treats you with contempt, you never quite forget it. So if we want to solve the problem of polarization today, we have to solve the contempt problem.

I sometimes collaborate on writing projects with the Dalai Lama. Recently, I was thinking about this contempt problem, and I said, "Your Holiness, what do I do when I feel contempt?" He said, "Practice warm-heartedness."

I started thinking about it, and it's true. When I do that; when we do that; when we have leaders who can do that, it's utterly world-changing. You can show true strength, if the next time you hear contempt, you answer with warm-heartedness.

Every single one of us is going to have an opportunity on social media or in person to answer somebody's contempt. So, are you going to do the right thing and make the world a little bit better; show your strength; and try to make your enemies your friends? Or are you going to make the problem worse? That's a question that each of us gets to answer—probably in the next twenty-four hours.

In the following chapter, I'll tell you more about that conversation with the Dalai Lama, but here I want to share one other thing about that little video: It got eleven million views on the Internet. Look, I'm not a famous celebrity or the president of the United States. I'm a fifty-four-year-old guy who runs a think tank, and I was giving a lecture at Harvard. Eleven million views is *a lot*.

From those two videos, I had a decent little market test—a sixty-eight-million-view sample that tells me the culture of contempt isn't what millions of us want. I realized we could fight back against that culture, if we just knew how.

And thus this book was born.

You might be getting the impression that this is yet another one of those books calling for more civility in our political discourse and tolerance of differing points of view. It isn't. Those standards are pitifully low. Don't believe it? Tell people, "My spouse and I are civil to each other," and they'll tell you to get counseling. Or say, "My coworkers tolerate me," and they'll ask how your job search is going.

I want something more radical and subversive than civility and tolerance, something that speaks to my heart's desire—the first word in this book's title: love. And not just love for friends and those who agree with me, but rather, love for those who disagree with me as well.

Maybe "love" sounds goofy to you, as if I were some kind of hippie (of which I have been credibly accused), or were suggesting an impossible philosophical ideal. The problem here is not the concept of love per se but its impoverished definition in our popular discourse. People today generally define love as an emotion—an intense feeling. That's hardly the solid basis for a program of national renewal. When I talk about love in this book, I am describing not something fuzzy and sentimental but clear and bracing. In his *Summa Theologica*, Saint Thomas Aquinas said, "To love is to will the good of the other."[10] The modern philosopher Michael Novak refines this further by adding two words: "To love is to will the good of the other *as other*" (emphasis mine).[11] He continues: "Love is not sentimental, nor restful in illusions, but watchful, alert, and ready to follow evidence. It seeks the real as lungs crave air." Exactly right. When

I call for a standard of love, I am asking us all to listen to our hearts, of course. But also to think clearly, look at the facts, and do difficult things when necessary, so that we can truly lift people up and bring them together.

So love isn't soft or silly. But love for whom? Love for your friends—that's easy. Love for strangers? Doable. But to love your enemies? Maybe this seems impossible to you. You might say, "There are some who are simply beyond the pale. There are millions of awful people in this country who advocate ideas that we cannot tolerate. They deserve our contempt, not our love!" I have heard this sentiment from serious journalists, respected academics, and mainstream politicians. I have thought it myself.

That attitude is both wrong and dangerously radical. Anyone who can't tell the difference between an ordinary Bernie Sanders supporter and a Stalinist revolutionary, or between Donald Trump's average voter and a Nazi, is either willfully ignorant or needs to get out of the house more. Today, our public discourse is shockingly hyperbolic in ascribing historically murderous ideologies to the tens of millions of ordinary Americans with whom we strongly disagree. Just because you disagree with something doesn't mean it's hate speech or the person saying it is a deviant.

Furthermore, this contempt is based on a mistaken

assumption—that there is no room for common ground, so there is no reason *not* to polarize with insults. Think about Hawk and Tommy. If you are a strong conservative and you saw Hawk with his fist in the air at the beginning of the rally, might he not look to you like the worst kind of radical revolutionary, undeserving of any consideration? If you are a strong progressive, how would Tommy look to you, alongside his fellow demonstrators in groups like Bikers for Trump? Like someone beyond all reason? And yet, through a bit of serendipitous decency, look what happened.

OK, you're probably thinking, but what about the odd people out there who really are Stalinists and Nazis? These are people at the absolute fringes who propagate conspiracy theories, hate, and racism—who in normal times would be dismissed as the tinfoil-hat crowd but capture public attention in the current contemptuous environment. Some do it under their own names; others are anonymous. What do we do about them?

Let's start with social media trolls. I get my share of haters on Twitter, from both the left and right. They are almost always anonymous, and many, no doubt, are not even real people, but instead are bots generating controversial content. I argue throughout this book that you should never be anonymous or engage with anonymous interlocutors. Engagement with love is a human endeavor, and requires us to be, and deal with, real people—not disembodied messages.

And the people who say these things openly? There is a tendency to revert to the old joke that if you wrestle a pig, you get muddy and the pig likes it. But ignoring voices of hate is a mistake. If we do, the ideas go unchallenged by people of goodwill. And if these people have views that are truly worthy of contempt? Remember that their *views* might be, but that no *person* is. Repudiate their views, confidently and concisely, with respect.

Finally, there is a practical, albeit self-interested, reason to avoid contempt, even for those with whom you disagree most strongly. It's horrible for you. You will see in this book that contempt makes you unhappy, unhealthy, and unattractive even to those who agree with you. Hating others is associated with depression. Contempt will wreck your relationships and harm your health. It is a dangerous vice, like smoking or drinking too much.

My point is simple: love and warm-heartedness might not change every heart and mind, but they are always worth trying, and they will always make *you* better off. They should be your (and my) default position.

Easier said than done, of course. It isn't the "factory setting" for many people, especially when nearly the whole culture is pushing in the opposite direction.

That's why I have written this book—to show you *how*. In it, you will find cutting-edge research from neuro-science, social science, history, and philosophy. You will meet the most visionary leaders in politics, business, media, and academia. I will show that without a mol-ecule of mushy moderation, people can become not just warriors for their point of view but healers in their com-munities. You will see why the current model of con-temptuous leadership is a losing proposition in the long run, as well as why better, not less, disagreement holds the key to greater harmony.

"OK," you say, "but I'm not a politician or CEO." Tommy and Hawk aren't either. They are pretty ordi-nary Americans. It's regular citizens acting as leaders who matter most in the battle against the culture of con-tempt. You see, whether or not we want to admit it, po-litical contempt and division are what economists call a demand-driven phenomenon. Famous people purvey it, but ordinary citizens are the ones creating a market for it. Think of it like methamphetamine: People who cook it and sell it are doing a terrible thing, and they should stop—but why they do it is no surprise: there's a lot of money in it. (Later, by the way, you will see that this comparison is not far-fetched. People are addicted to drugs and contempt in similar neurological ways.)

All this means we can't wait for our leaders to change;

we need to lead the rebellion ourselves. While we can't single-handedly change the country, we can change ourselves. By declaring our independence from the bitterness washing over our nation, each of us can strike a small blow for greater national harmony, and become happier in the process.

The story of Hawk and Tommy is a metaphor for America—I hope. The events of that day started with contempt but ended with warm-heartedness. Two groups that could hardly be more different overcame their mutual disdain and, without coming to political agreement, still found common cause in their shared humanity and desire for lives of liberty and happiness.

The purpose of this book is simple: to help an America that currently looks like the beginning of the Mother of All Rallies reach a place where it looks more like the rally's end. Rather than achieving harmony by accident, as seemed to happen at the rally that day in Washington, I hope this book will help each of us get there on purpose.

So if you are ready to rebel alongside me against the culture of contempt, if you are hungry for a country where people can disagree without bitterness and hatred, if you want to subvert the power of the contempt-mongers, then I have written this book for you.

And if for some reason you don't agree that our

national discourse is in grave crisis, I have written it for you, too. If you read the book, I think there's a chance I might change your mind about what's best for you and for the country. Furthermore, I am convinced that by following the ideas and rules in this book, you will be a happier, healthier, more persuasive person.

This book is not an attempt to change your politics. I have strong views and you probably do, too. Most likely, we disagree on some things. My point in this book is not that you need to change your political outlook, but that I need you all the more if you disagree with me, because our disagreement—if we do it right—is what makes our country strong.

Overcoming a culture of contempt will require more than a rousing chorus of "Kumbaya" and a basket of platitudes. Building real harmony in the face of difference and disagreement is hard work. Americans will have to be willing, as Hawk and Tommy were, to share a stage—sometimes literally—with those on the opposite end of the political spectrum. Nevertheless, equipped with a new outlook on our culture, a better approach to leadership, the right tools of communication, and a healthy dose of courage, we can bridge the political divides that have proliferated across the country in recent years.

Will we win every heart? Of course not. Nothing

could get 100 percent of the population. But I believe the majority of Americans love the country and have love for one another. We just have to build a movement and culture around these truths.

Let's get started.

Chapter 1
The Culture of Contempt

The year was 2006. I was a professor at Syracuse University, and I had just released my first commercial book, *Who Really Cares*. It was about charitable giving—about the people in America who give the most to charity, broken down by categories such as politics and religion.

Sounds like a real page-turner, doesn't it? Frankly, I didn't expect it to get much attention. I would have been happy if it had sold a couple thousand copies. Why? My past work had consisted mostly of dense academic journal articles with blood-pumping titles like "Genetic Algorithms and Public Economics" and "Contingent Valuation and the Winner's Curse in Internet Art Auctions." *Who Really Cares* was a little more interesting, but not much. I published the book, and waited for the phone to not ring.

Instead, it rang. And rang. As sometimes happens with academic books, it hit the popular zeitgeist in just the right way. For whatever reason, it was a hot news story that some people gave a lot to charity and some didn't, and my book appeared to explain why. A few famous people talked about the book, and before I knew it, I was on TV and the book started selling hundreds of copies a day.

Weirdest of all for me, total strangers began to reach out. I quickly got used to e-mails from people I had never met, pouring out intimate details of their lives, because, I learned, when people read a whole book by you, they feel that they know you. Moreover, if they don't like the book, they don't like *you*.

One afternoon a couple of weeks after the book came out, I got an e-mail from a man in Texas that began "Dear Professor Brooks: You are a fraud." Tough start. But my Texan correspondent didn't stop there. His e-mail was about five thousand words long, criticizing in vitriolic detail every chapter in the book and informing me of my numerous inadequacies as a researcher and person. It took me twenty minutes just to get through his screed.

OK now, put yourself in my position. What would you do at this point? Here are three options:

Option 1. Ignore him. He's just some random guy, right? Why waste *my* time, even if he wasted *his* lambasting my book, chapter and verse?

Option 2. Insult him. Say, "Get a life, man. Don't you have something better to do than reach out and bother a stranger?"

Option 3. Destroy him. Pick out three or four of his most glaring, idiotic errors and throw them in his face, adding, "Hey, blockhead, if you don't know economics, best not to embarrass yourself in front of a professional economist."

More and more, these three alternatives (or a combination of them) are the only ones we feel are available to us in modern ideological conflicts. Few other options come to mind when we're confronted with disagreement. Notice that they all grow from the same root: contempt. They all express the view that my interlocutor is unworthy of my consideration.

Each option will provoke a different response, but what they all have in common is that they foreclose the possibility of a productive discussion. They basically guarantee permanent enmity. You might note that *he started it*. True—although you could probably say I started it by writing the book. Either way, just as the rejoinder "he started it" never cut any ice for me when my kids were little and fighting in the back seat of the car, it has no moral weight here, where our goal is to undercut the culture of contempt.

Later, I'll tell you which of the three options—ignore, insult, or destroy—I chose in responding to my Texan correspondent. But before I do so, we have a trip to make through the science and philosophy of contempt.

In 2014, researchers at Northwestern University, Boston College, and the University of Melbourne published an article in the *Proceedings of the National Academy of Sciences,* a prestigious academic journal.[1] The subject was human conflict due to "motive attribution asymmetry"—the phenomenon of assuming that your ideology is based in love, while your opponent's ideology is based in hate.

The researchers found that a majority of Republicans and Democrats today suffer from a level of motive attribution asymmetry that is comparable to that of Palestinians and Israelis. In both cases, the two sides think that they are driven by benevolence, while the other side is evil and motivated by hate. Therefore neither side is willing to negotiate or compromise. As a result, the authors found, "political conflict between American Democrats and Republicans and ethnoreligious conflict between Israelis and Palestinians seem intractable, despite the availability of reasonable compromise solutions in both cases."

Think about what this means: We are headed to the point where achieving bipartisan compromise, on issues from immigration to guns to confirming a Supreme Court justice, is as difficult as achieving Middle East peace. We may not be engaging in daily violence against each other, but we can't make progress as a society when both sides believe that they are motivated by love while the other side is motivated by hate.

People often characterize the current moment as being "angry." I wish this were true, because anger tends to be self-limiting. It is an emotion that occurs when we want to change someone's behavior and believe we can do so. While anger is often perceived as a negative emotion, research shows that its social purpose is not actually to drive others away but rather to remove problematic elements of a relationship and bring people back together.[2] Believe it or not, there is little evidence that anger in marriage is correlated with separation or divorce.[3]

Think about a fight you've had with a close friend, sibling, or spouse. If you were upset and got angry, was your goal to push her out of your life entirely? Did you suppose that the person was motivated by her *hatred* for you? Of course not. Whether anger is the right strategy or not, we get angry because we recognize that things are not as they should be, we want to set them right, and we think we can.

Motive attribution asymmetry doesn't lead to anger, because it doesn't make you want to repair the relationship. Believing your foe is motivated by hate leads to something far worse: contempt. While anger seeks to bring someone back into the fold, contempt seeks to exile. It attempts to mock, shame, and permanently exclude from relationships by belittling, humiliating, and ignoring. So while anger says, "I care about this," contempt says, "You disgust me. You are beneath caring about."

Once I asked a psychologist friend about the root of violent conflict. He told me it was "contempt that is poorly hidden." What makes you violent is the perception that you are being held in contempt. This rips families, communities, and whole nations apart. If you want to make a lifelong enemy, show him contempt.

The destructive power of contempt is well documented in the work of the famous social psychologist and relationship expert John Gottman. He is a longtime professor at the University of Washington in Seattle and cofounder with his wife, Julie Schwartz Gottman, of the Gottman Institute, which is dedicated to improving relationships. In his work, Gottman has studied thousands of married couples. He'll ask each couple to tell their story—how they met and courted, their highs and lows as a couple, and how their marriage has changed over the years—before having them discuss contentious issues.

After watching a couple interact for just one hour, he can predict with *94 percent accuracy* whether that couple will divorce within three years.[4] How can he tell? It's not from the anger that the couples express. Gottman confirms that anger doesn't predict separation or divorce.[5] The biggest warning signs, he explains, are indicators of *contempt*. These include sarcasm, sneering, hostile humor, and—worst of all—eye-rolling. These little acts effectively say "You are worthless" to the one person you should love more than any other. Want to see if a couple will end up in divorce court? Watch them discuss a contentious topic, and see if either partner rolls his or her eyes.

What does all this have to do with American politics? I asked him that. At this question, Gottman—an ebullient, happy person—becomes somber.

There's been a denigration of respect in the dialogue in this country. It's always us versus them. . . . We see Republicans thinking they're better than Democrats, Democrats thinking they're better than Republicans, people from the coast thinking they're better than people inland. It goes on and on, and I think it's very harmful. This "us versus them" is what gets our medial prefrontal cortex—that's the part of the brain between our eyes—to not respond with understanding and compassion. And that's not what our country's about.

The pandemic of contempt in political matters makes it impossible for people of opposing views to work together. Go to YouTube and watch the 2016 presidential debates: they are masterpieces of eye-rolling, sarcasm, and sneering derision. For that matter, listen as politicians at all levels talk about their election opponents, or members of the other party. Increasingly, they describe people unworthy of any kind of consideration, with no legitimate ideas or views. And social media? On any contentious subject, these platforms are contempt machines.

Of course this is self-defeating in a nation in which political competitors must also be collaborators. How likely are you to want to work with someone who has told an audience that you are a fool or a criminal? Would you make a deal with someone who publicly said you are corrupt? How about becoming friends with someone who says your opinions are idiotic? Why would you be willing to compromise politically with such a person? You can resolve problems with someone with whom you disagree, even if you disagree angrily, but you can't come to a solution with someone who holds you in contempt or for whom you have contempt.

Contempt is impractical and bad for a country dependent on people working together in politics, communities, and the economy. Unless we hope to become a one-party state, we cannot afford contempt for our fellow Americans who simply disagree with us.

Nor is contempt morally justified. The vast majority of Americans on the other side of the ideological divide are not terrorists or criminals. They are people like us who happen to see certain contentious issues differently. When we treat our fellow Americans as enemies, we lose friendships, and thus, love and happiness. That's exactly what's happening. I already cited a poll showing that a sixth of Americans have stopped talking to a family member or close friend because of the 2016 election. People have ended close relationships, the most important source of happiness, because of politics.

In one particularly sad example of this in the run-up

to the 2018 midterm election, *six siblings* of an incumbent congressman made a television advertisement for his opponent.[6] One sister called him a racist. A brother said, "He just doesn't appear to be well." Another brother impugned his motives for his policies, saying his views on regulation must be motivated by money from industry. The congressman's public response? His siblings "are related by blood to me but like leftists everywhere, they put political ideology before family. Stalin would be proud."[7]

In 1960, only 5 percent of Americans said they would be displeased if their child married someone from the other political party. By 2010, that number was 40 percent, and no doubt has risen from there.[8] We have become far removed indeed from Thomas Jefferson's admonition that a "difference in politics should never be permitted to enter into social intercourse, or to disturb its friendships, its charities or justice."[9]

Gottman calls contempt "sulfuric acid for love." However, it doesn't just destabilize our relationships and our politics. Gottman tells me that it also causes a comprehensive degradation of our immune systems. It damages self-esteem, alters behavior, and even impairs cognitive processing.[10] According to the American Psychological Association, the feeling of rejection, so often experienced after being treated with contempt, increases "anxiety, depression, jealousy, and sadness" and "reduces performance on difficult intellectual tasks."[11] Being treated with contempt takes a measurable physical toll. Those who routinely feel excluded "have poorer sleep quality, and their immune systems don't function as well" as those of people who don't suffer contemptuous treatment.[12]

As important, contempt isn't just harmful for the person being treated poorly. It is also harmful for the contemptuous person, because treating others with contempt causes us to secrete two stress hormones, cortisol and adrenaline. The consequence of constantly secreting these hormones—the equivalent of living under significant consistent stress—is staggering. Gottman points out that people in couples who are constantly battling die *twenty years earlier*, on average, than those who consistently seek mutual understanding. Our contempt is inarguably disastrous for *us*, let alone the people we are holding in contempt.

In truth, contempt is *not* what we really want. How do I know this? To begin with, that's what I hear all day, every day. I travel constantly, and for my job I talk about policy and politics. Not a day goes by when someone doesn't bemoan the fact that we are coming apart as a country, unable to have a respectful airing of political views like civilized adults. People are exhausted.

That's exactly what Tim Dixon, cofounder of the organization More in Common, calls the "exhausted majority": Americans who are tired of the constant conflict and worried about the future of the country. In a groundbreaking study on political attitudes in the US, he finds that 93 percent of Americans say that they are tired of how divided we have become as a country; 71 percent believe this "strongly." Large majorities say privately that they believe in the importance of compromise, reject the absolutism of the extreme wings of both parties, and are not motivated by partisan loyalty.[13]

A lot of other evidence backs up Dixon's claim that a majority of Americans dislike the culture of contempt. A 2017 *Washington Post*–University of Maryland poll asked, "Do you think problems in America's politics right now are similar to most periods of partisan disagreement, or do you think problems have reached a dangerous low point?" Seventy-one percent of respondents chose the latter.[14] Almost two-thirds of Americans say that the future of the country is a very or somewhat significant source of stress, more than the percentage who say they are stressed by money concerns or work.[15] Even more disconcerting, 60 percent of Americans consider our current political moment the lowest point in U.S. history that they can remember—a figure, the American Psychological Association points out, that spans "every generation, including those who lived through World War II and Vietnam, the Cuban missile crisis and the September 11 terrorist attacks."[16] More than 70 percent of Americans believe that the country will be greatly hurt if opposing parties don't work together.[17]

This defies the idea that America is split between two big groups of hyperpartisans intent on vanquishing the other side. On the contrary, most are quite nuanced in their views and don't fit into a neat ideological camp. As just one illustrative example, Dixon's exhausted majority is significantly more likely than the highly partisan minority to believe that hate speech in America is a problem, but that political correctness is *also* a problem. In other words, this majority wants our country to address the former, but not by embracing the latter.

You might be thinking I have some explaining to do here. On the one hand, I am asserting that our culture, especially our political culture, is overrun with contempt. On the other hand, I'm saying it's not what a pretty big majority of us want. But don't we get what we want in democracies and free markets?

Yes and no. There are lots of cases in which people

demand something they hate. Have you ever met a problem drinker? Every morning, he berates himself for his lack of self-discipline and resolves not to drink that night. When night rolls around, filled with anxiety and cravings, he says, "Eh, I'll quit tomorrow." Similarly, most smokers say they wish they didn't smoke, yet they voluntarily continue, spending their money and wrecking their health in the process.

What's going on here? The answer is addiction, of course. Addiction clouds our ability to make long-run choices in our own interest. Personally, I have a terrible sweet tooth. I know perfectly well that I should cut refined sugar out of my diet. I *want* to get off the sweet stuff. But I just know that tonight, around eight p.m., I'll lose my resolve and hit the Oreos. (It's my wife's fault for buying them.) You probably have your own weakness, out of which you demand something in the short run that you don't really want in the long run. Maybe it's a bad relationship you just can't quit, or gambling, or buying clothes you can't afford.

Economists carve out a special sort of demand for addictive things. They note that we make decisions that are deeply suboptimal in the long run because the pain of breaking the habit is so high in the short run. Therefore, we really wish we didn't drink, but we put off the discomfort of quitting, day after day.

America is addicted to political contempt. While most of us hate what it is doing to our country and worry about how contempt coarsens our culture over the long term, many of us still compulsively consume the ideological equivalent of meth from elected officials, academics, entertainers, and some of the news media. Millions actively indulge their habit by participating in the cycle of contempt in the way they treat others, especially on social media. We wish our national debates were nutritious and substantive, but we have an insatiable craving for insults to the other side. As much as we know we should ignore the nasty columnist, turn off the TV loudmouth, and stop checking our Twitter feeds, we indulge our guilty urge to listen as our biases are confirmed that the other guys are not just wrong, but stupid and evil.

We are responsible for our contempt addiction, of course, just as meth addicts are ultimately accountable for their addiction. But there are also our pushers—the political meth dealers. Knowing our weakness, dividing leaders on both the left and right seek power and fame by setting American against American, brother against brother, compatriot against compatriot. These leaders assert that we must choose sides, then argue that the other side is wicked—not worthy of any consideration—rather than challenging them to listen to others with kindness and respect. They foster a culture of contempt.

There is an "outrage industrial complex" in American media today, which profits handsomely from our contempt addiction. This starts by catering to just one ideological side. Leaders and media on the left and right then keep their audiences hooked on contempt by telling audiences what they want to hear, selling a narrative of conflict and painting gross caricatures of the other side. They make us feel justified in our own beliefs while affirming our worst assumptions about those who disagree with us—namely that they are, in fact, stupid, evil, and not worth giving the time of day.

In a battle for public attention, elite opinion makers on both the right and left increasingly describe our political disagreements as an apocalyptic struggle between good and evil, comparing the other side to animals and using metaphors of terrorism. Open your favorite newspaper or browse the prime-time cable lineup and you will find example after example. The result of hyperbolic rhetoric becoming commonplace? A deepening culture of contempt, a growing threat of actual violence, and—of course—record profits. (Hey, you saw *Breaking Bad*, right? Meth is very profitable, too.)

Social media intensifies our addiction by allowing us to filter out the news and opinions we disagree with, thus purifying the contempt drug. According to the Brookings Institution, the average Facebook user has five politically like-minded friends for every friend on the other side of the political spectrum.[18] Researchers from the University of Georgia have shown that Twitter users are unlikely to be exposed to cross-ideological content because the users they follow are politically homogeneous.[19] Even in the world of dating apps, scholars have found that people sort themselves based on political affiliation.[20] These companies give us platforms to create feedback loops where we are exposed only to those who think similarly, and where people can hide behind a cloak of anonymity and spew hateful, vitriolic commentary.

"Ideological siloing" means we stop interacting entirely with those who hold opposing views. Polls show that a majority of both Republicans and Democrats have "just a few" or no friends who are members of the other party.[21] By contrast, just 14 percent of Republicans and 9 percent of Democrats have "a lot" of close friends from the opposing party.[22] The results of not knowing people of opposing viewpoints and seeing them only through the lens of hostile media is predictable. Today, 55 percent of Democrats have a "very unfavorable" view of Republicans, and 58 percent of Republicans hold that view of Democrats. This represents a threefold increase since 1994.[23]

There is evidence that as we become less exposed to opposing viewpoints, we become less logically competent as people. Author David Blankenhorn has noted a rise in several modes of weak political thinking in the past decade.[24] Notable among these modes are: extreme binary opinions ("I am completely right, so you are completely wrong"); seeing any uncertainty as a mark of weakness; motivated reasoning (looking only for evidence that supports your own opinion—which is easier when one can curate one's news and social media); *argumentum ad hominem* ("You have selfish and immoral reasons for your opinion"); and a refusal to agree on any basic facts ("Your news is fake news").

The structure of party politics is also driving the culture of contempt. Every two years, 435 seats in the House of Representatives are up for election. In the last three national elections, more and more of those seats have become noncompetitive, with incumbents winning reelection at rates of 90 percent, 95 percent, and 97 percent.[25] Both political parties draw up gerrymandered districts that are filled with true believers, dividing theirs into many districts and lumping opponents into few so as to decrease their legislative representation. As a result, politicians increasingly have to appeal only to members of their own party for votes. Primaries often devolve into a competition to see who can take the most extreme positions in order to prove party fealty and turn out the hard-core base. The inevitable result is the demonization of the other side.

Members of Congress often say that a big change over the past decade is that they no longer spend much social time with members of the opposing party. Not only do they disagree about politics; they hardly know one another as people. You have probably heard many times that in decades past, Democrats and Republicans would argue vigorously on the floor by day, and then go out to dinner together by night. This was part of how they ultimately got business done. By sharing life together outside of work, they developed the trust and goodwill necessary to make difficult choices for the good of all, including those beyond their own political camps.

Politicians often tell me they have felt the need to avoid these friendships for self-preservation; they worry about being seen as too chummy with the other side. In an environment of gerrymandered ideological purity and extreme political contempt, a primary challenger's dream is finding an incumbent fraternizing with the "enemy."

This isn't bad for just our politics; it's bad for politicians as people. Of course, some politicians on both sides like the polarized status quo—it has made their careers possible. Perhaps I would have believed this is the norm before I moved to Washington, DC, ten years ago, but today I know that's not the case at all. I have gotten to know many members of Congress as friends, and—as surprising as it might seem to some readers—my admiration for politicians has grown enormously. They are some of the most patriotic, hardworking people I have ever met. They love America and hate our culture of contempt as much as you and I. They tell me they regret how polarized things have become and wish they knew how to fight the trend. Like us, they are victims of America's political contempt addiction.

One of their biggest regrets is that important issues that require cooperation become a political Ping-Pong match. One side gains power and imposes its vision on strict party-line voting, and then the other side gains power and tries to impose its vision in the same way. The people caught in the middle are those with the least power.

Take health care in America. The Affordable Care Act of 2010—aka Obamacare—changed how health care was purchased and delivered for millions of low-income Americans. It was passed on party-line Democratic votes in the House and Senate, with no Republican support at all. This, of course, set it up to be rolled back the minute the Republicans took over both houses and the White House, which they did in 2016. While getting rid of Obamacare proved harder than Republicans planned, they did succeed in dismantling large parts of it, once again changing how poorer Americans got their health care, and doing so on strict party-line terms. No one doubts that when (not *if*) the Democrats take full control once again, the political Ping-Pong match will continue, wherein low-income Americans' health care is the ball.

As an old African proverb has it, "When elephants fight, it's the grass that suffers." The weak get hurt in conflicts between the powerful. Americans at the bottom of the income scale are always the ones who lose when contempt crowds out cooperation at the top. The politics of contempt never hurts the rich very much. It hurts people in poverty. We should all be able to agree that that's bad.

Contempt is driving us apart and making us miserable. It is holding us hostage. What exactly do we want instead?

For the answer to this, let me start by turning back to my opening story—about my correspondent in Texas who hated my book and let me know in vivid terms. My response options seemed to be (1) ignore, (2) insult, or (3) destroy.

Instead, I accidentally picked a fourth option, and it created a huge epiphany for me. Here's what happened: As I read his e-mail, I was insulted and felt attacked. But I also kept thinking, *He read my book!* I was filled with gratitude. As an academic, I was used to writing things that almost no one would read. I had put my whole heart into that project for two years, and this guy had taken the time to read the whole thing. That amazed me. I became conscious of that particular sentiment, and for whatever reason, I decided to tell him that. I wrote back and said I realized he really hated my book, but that it had taken me a lot of work to write, and I deeply appreciated his time and attention to every detail.

Fifteen minutes later, a second message from the guy popped up in my in-box. I opened the e-mail and braced myself. But instead of another salvo, he said he was shocked that I'd read his note and the next time I was in Dallas we should grab some dinner. This message was completely friendly. From enemy to friend in a matter of minutes! Did he suddenly like my book? Of course not. He simply learned that he liked *me* because I had taken the time to read his e-mail and was nice in the way I responded.

Don't get the wrong impression here. I'm not some saint who always reacts that way when personally attacked. Perhaps our unexpected rapprochement that day was just dumb luck. But here's what I learned from that lucky interaction: contempt is no match for love. The cycle of contempt depended on me, and I broke it with just a few words of gratitude. Doing so felt great for me, and it changed another person's heart.

I saw firsthand that contempt transmuted into friendliness when it was met with an overt expression of kindness and respect. From this, I saw for myself that kindness, reconciliation, and connection—not contempt, division, and isolation—are what our hearts really desire. I have since sought to understand the science behind this, reading all the scholarship I could find, and getting to know scholars on this topic.

One of the leading experts is Matthew Lieberman, a social psychologist at the University of California–Los Angeles. Lieberman has spent decades exploring the neuroscience of human relationships. He contends that we have an innate desire for positive social connections with one another, and that our brains experience deep pleasure when we achieve these connections.

You can think about this in dollars and cents. In his book, *Social: Why Our Brains Are Wired to Connect*, Lieberman observes that simply having a friend you see on most days gives the equivalent happiness boost of earning an additional $100,000 of income each year.[26] Seeing your neighbors on a regular basis gives as much happiness as an extra $60,000. Meanwhile, the experience of breaking a critical social tie, such as with a family member, is like experiencing a large income decline.[27] I suppose the congressman I mentioned before (who was denounced by his six siblings) effectively suffered bankruptcy.

In a similar study, psychologists from Brigham Young University examined the habits and social connections of more than three hundred thousand participants, and found that a lack of strong relationships increases the risk of premature death from all causes by 50 percent.[28] A Harvard University publication notes that this lack of communion through social connections is roughly equivalent in health effects to that of smoking fifteen cigarettes a day.[29]

Here's what these facts and figures mean to you and me. We all want to earn a lot more, and no one wants a big loss in income. We can't always control that, but we can affect something just as valuable for our well-being: our connections with others. Would you trade away $100,000 of your salary, or years of healthy life, over a political disagreement? Probably not. So don't sacrifice a friendship or family relationship over one either, and don't pass up a possible new friendship just because of politics.

A number of recent studies have asked why we crave

connection and have found physiological answers. As neuroscientists from Emory University have discovered, social cooperation activates the parts of our brain that are linked to reward processing.[30] Using brain scans, they demonstrate that when we experience the pleasure of connection, these reward circuits are activated, proving that "social cooperation is intrinsically rewarding to the human brain."[31] By contrast, when we experience exclusion or rejection, the brain's pain centers are activated. In fact, the brain processes relational rejection the same way it processes physical pain. As Lieberman has found in his research, a broken heart can in many ways feel like a broken leg.[32]

Once again, ask yourself: Would I be willing to break a bone to be "right," politically?

We probably shouldn't need brain scans to tell us that building relationships is far preferable to the consequences of contempt and division. After all, the great thinkers and religions of the world have been counseling the wisdom of unity for millennia.

In Plato's *Republic*, the great philosopher writes, "Can there be any greater evil than discord and distraction and plurality where unity ought to reign? Or any greater good than the bond of unity? There cannot."[33] Aristotle believed the same thing. If separated from the unifying bonds of friendship, he wrote in his

Nicomachean Ethics, "no one would choose to live, though he had all other goods."[34]

This theme is consistent throughout the sacred texts of the world's religions, too. Psalm 133 proclaims, "How good and pleasant it is when God's people live together in unity!"[35] In Matthew's Gospel, Jesus warns, "Every kingdom divided against itself will be ruined, and every city or household divided against itself will not stand."[36] And the Bhagavad Gita, one of the ancient holy books of Hinduism, teaches that knowledge that "sees in all things a single, imperishable being, undivided among the divided" is *sattvic*—meaning pure, good, and virtuous.[37]

The Founding Fathers knew that social harmony would form the backbone of America. In his celebrated pamphlet *Common Sense*, Thomas Paine held that "it is not in numbers, but in unity, that our great strength lies."[38] James Madison, in the fourteenth Federalist Paper, warned that the "most alarming of all novelties, the most wild of all projects, the most rash of all attempts, is that of rendering us in pieces, in order to preserve our liberties and promote our happiness."[39] John Adams believed that the cancer of faction in America was to be "dreaded as the greatest political Evil, under our Constitution."[40] In his farewell address, George Washington famously warned against "the baneful effects" of political enmity.[41]

We try to have it both ways, of course—love for our friends and contempt for our enemies. Indeed, sometimes we even try to build unity around the common bonds of contempt for "the other." But it doesn't work, any more than an alcoholic can have "just a little drink" to take the edge off. Drunkenness crowds out sobriety. Contempt crowds out love because it becomes our focus. If you have contempt for "them," more and more people will become "them." Monty Python made this point hilariously in the movie *Life of Brian*, where the bitterest of enemies are two rival Jewish dissident groups: the Judean People's Front and the People's Front of Judea.

From the philosophers of ancient Greece to the world's great religions to our own Founding Fathers to the psychology research of the modern era, we are exhorted to choose our heart's true desire: love and kindness. All warn unambiguously that division, if allowed to take permanent root, will be our misery and downfall.

Two caveats are in order here. First, unity does not necessarily mean agreement. I will devote a whole chapter later in this book to the importance of respectful *dis*agreement. Second, unity is always an aspiration; we will never be 100 percent unified. Even in times of war, our nation has not been unanimously behind the effort.

Nevertheless, though not perfectly attainable, the goal to be *more* unified is still the right one to give us more of what we want as people.

We want love. How do we get it? We have to start by saying that it *is* what we really want. That is easier said than done. A famous Bible story makes this point:

> As Jesus and his disciples, together with a large crowd, were leaving the city, a blind man, Bartimaeus, was sitting by the roadside begging. When he heard that it was Jesus of Nazareth, he began to shout, "Jesus, Son of David, have mercy on me!" . . . "What do you want me to do for you?" Jesus asked him. The blind man said, "Rabbi, I want to see."[42]

At first, it seems kind of silly. A blind man, Bartimaeus, wants a miracle from Jesus. Jesus asks, "What do you want?" As my kids might say, "Duh—he wants to see." And, in fact, that is pretty much what the blind man answers.

This story is profound because, while people *do* know what they really want, they often *don't* ask for it. Think about the last time you had a real conflict with someone you love. You badly wanted the conflict to end and affection to return, but you kept fighting anyway. I have a friend who didn't talk to his daughter for twenty years and didn't even know his grandchildren's names. He badly wanted to reconcile but couldn't bring himself to do it. Maybe you have never done anything this extreme, but at one time or another, we have all experienced the pain of a relational fracture that our pride prevents us from fixing.

Once again, there's the addiction. Addicts *all* want to be free from addiction, and there is a lot of help out there to set them free. All they have to do is let go of the thing they hate, and ask for what they truly want. But they don't, sometimes even until death. Why not? Most say the short-term agony of quitting is just too great, or that booze or other drugs, as terrible as they are, are the only thing that give real satisfaction in an empty life.

We have a cultural addiction to contempt—an addiction abetted by the outrage industrial complex for profit and power—and it's tearing us apart. Most of us don't want that, though. We want love, kindness, and respect. *But* we have to ask for it, choose it. It's hard; we are prideful, and contempt can give a sense of short-term purpose and satisfaction, like one more drink. No one ever said that breaking an addiction was easy. But make no mistake: Like Bartimaeus, we *can* choose what we truly want, as individuals and as a nation.

How? It's not good enough to leave it up to chance,

hoping we accidentally react as I did to my Texan e-mailer, or as Hawk Newsome and Tommy Hodges did on the Mall in Washington, DC. What can we do starting today to reject contempt and embrace love?

For an answer, I asked two experts.

The first is Dr. John Gottman, whom we met earlier in this chapter. I asked him how he thought we could use his ideas on marital harmony to improve our national discourse. If you want a more unified America based on bonds of love, how should you treat others with whom you disagree politically?

Gottman paused when I asked him this, because he had never answered this question before. Professors are always reluctant to go outside the range of their data and specific expertise. Nevertheless, he told me that he loved America, was brokenhearted by the contempt spreading across the country, and wanted to bring us back together. So he gave me four rules:

1. Focus on other people's distress, and focus on it empathetically. When others are upset about politics, listen to them respectfully. Try to understand their point of view before offering your own. Never listen only to rebut.

2. In your interactions with others, particularly in areas of disagreement, adopt the "five-to-one

rule," which he gives couples. Make sure you offer five positive comments for every criticism. On social media, that means five positive messages for every one others might see as negative.

3. No contempt is *ever* justified, even if, in the heat of the moment, you think someone deserves it. It is unjustified more often than you know, it is always bad for you, and it will never convince anyone that she is wrong.

4. Go where people disagree with you and learn from them. That means making new friends and seeking out opinions you know you don't agree with. How to act when you get there? See rules 1 to 3!

These rules are so important that I will be expanding upon them (and others) for the rest of this book. If they seem hard to follow, don't worry! I'll show you how to do it.

The second person I consulted about how to fight contempt is the wisest man I know, who also happens to be one of the world's experts on bringing people together through bonds of compassion and love: His Holiness the Dalai Lama.

The Dalai Lama is the spiritual leader of the Tibetan

Buddhist people and one of the most respected leaders in the world today. We have had a collaboration for a number of years, and although I am a Catholic and not a Buddhist, for me he is a mentor and guide. I was visiting him at his monastery in Dharamshala, India, in the Himalayan foothills, when I was starting to work on this book. "Your Holiness," I asked him, "what do I do when I feel contempt?" As you already know from the introduction, he responded, "Practice warm-heartedness."

To be honest, at first I thought, *You got anything else?* It sounded more like an aphorism than useful counsel. But when I thought about it, I saw it was actually tough and practical advice. He was not advocating surrender to the views of those with whom we disagree. If I believe I am right, I have a duty to stick to my views. But my duty is also to be kind, fair, and friendly to all, even those with whom I have great differences.

Difficult? Sure. The Dalai Lama would be the first to note that warm-heartedness is for strong people, not weak people. It is advice he has taken himself. At the age of just fifteen, he became the leader of the Tibetan Buddhist people after China's invasion of Tibet in 1950.[43] Following brutal suppression of his people, the Dalai Lama escaped into exile in 1959, and has since led a poor and dispossessed Tibetan community from his home in Dharamshala. The Dalai Lama and his people have been treated with contempt worse than most of us will ever experience in our lives—driven from their homes and barely recognized as people.

How has he responded? The Dalai Lama begins each day by offering up prayers for China, its leaders, and its people.[44] He practices warm-heartedness toward the very regime that drove him and his followers into exile and continues to oppress the people of Tibet. That is strong, not weak. Warm-heartedness is not for the faint-hearted.

My next question to him was: How do I do that? Give me some practical tips, Your Holiness. He told me: Think back to a time in your life when you answered contempt with warm-heartedness. Remember how it made you feel, and then do it again. It was at that moment that I realized that warm-heartedness is exactly what transformed my e-mail exchange at the beginning of this chapter. I accidentally answered contempt with warm-heartedness and watched the contempt melt away in an instant.

Kindness and warm-heartedness are the antivenom for the poisonous contempt coursing through the veins of our political discourse. Contempt is what we saw when Tommy Hodges and Hawk Newsome—the Trump rally organizer and the Black Lives Matter activist we met at the start of this book—arrived on the National Mall. By inviting Hawk up onstage, Tommy did more than give Hawk a platform to speak. He acknowledged his dignity as a fellow American. He effectively said, *I may not agree with you, but what you have to say matters.* That simple demonstration of respect broke through the wall of mutual contempt that had separated them and completely transformed their interaction.

Hawk then responded in kind, by engaging his audience in a positive, warm-hearted way. He expressed moral common cause with his listeners—declaring that he was an American who loves his country and who wants to make America great—while challenging them to think differently about the plight of African Americans. His approach was deeply unifying. He made a moral case for compassion and fairness, and appealed to something that everyone had written on their hearts.

That doesn't mean that everyone in the audience agreed with what he said; they didn't. Something more profound happened than mere political agreement: a human connection that led to a respectful, productive competition of ideas.

This is exactly what America needs. It is what our hearts desire. And it does not have to be a flash in the pan. It's actually something that we can engineer and replicate all over America if we have the courage and will to do so.

How? Start with your own interactions. When you are treated with contempt, don't see it as a threat but as an opportunity. In the Dhammapada, one of the primary collections of the teachings of the Buddha, the master says:

Conquer anger through gentleness,
unkindness through kindness,
greed through generosity,
and falsehood by truth.[45]

When I first read that, I thought it was strange that the Buddha would instruct us to turn loving-kindness into an instrumentality to conquer others, but that was the wrong way of reading it. On reflection, I realized that *I* am the angry one, the ill-tempered one, the miser, and the liar. My job is to conquer *me*. My tool for doing so is to show warm-heartedness to others, especially when they are not showing it to me.

Your opportunity when treated with contempt is to change at least one heart—yours. You may not be able to control the actions of others, but you can absolutely control your reaction. *You* can break the cycle of contempt. You have the power to do that.

Your opportunity will come sooner than you think, whether on the left or right. Feel that you've been unfairly attacked on social media? Respond with warm-heartedness. Overhear someone make a snide remark about people who vote like you? Respond with kindness. Want to say something insulting about people who disagree with you? Take a breath, and show love instead.

That sounds great, you may be saying, but what if I don't feel it? *It doesn't matter.* As we'll see in the next chapter, it is what we *do* that most often determines how we *feel*, not the other way around. If you wait to feel warm-hearted toward your ideological foes, you may as well have WAITING TO FEEL WARM-HEARTED chiseled on your tombstone. Action doesn't follow attitude except in the rarest of circumstances. Rather, attitude follows action. Don't feel it? Fake it. Soon enough you'll start to feel it.

The rest of this book gives a lot of practical tips on how to answer contempt with warm-heartedness, how to choose kindness over contempt. It does a lot more than just leading each of us in our personal battle, however. It teaches each of us how we can be leaders who fight contempt in society and bring more people—no matter how they vote or see the world—to the joy of loving one another.

Chapter 2
Can You Afford to Be Nice?

It's a classic story. An average-looking guy—call him Michael—meets a beautiful woman. Despite the fact that she's slightly out of his league, she starts spending time with him and seems to like him. He makes her dinner, listens attentively to her, and treats her with unfailing respect. Things are going great until one day she meets a jerk—call him Todd—who treats her horribly but is handsome and confident. She falls in love with Todd and relegates poor Michael to the friend zone. He knows Todd won't treat her right and it probably won't end well, but that's no comfort at all.

This is the "nice guy's paradox," and it appears most people believe it really exists. Go to the self-help section of any bookstore and you'll see titles for men like *Stop Being the "Nice Guy": How to Get a Girlfriend*, and books for women like *Stop Dating Jerks!* If this is any indication, when it comes to romance, nice guys finish last.

The same goes for politics, and forget about the "guys" part—it goes for everyone. Want to be a winner in our culture of contempt? You can't be nice, because that's *weak*. Look at the bestselling books on politics, and you will find a lineup of titles about the other side—whichever that happens to be—being liars, crooks, traitors, and crazies. Furthermore, in the ultimate political market test—elections—do we see any evidence at all these days that being a peach is a winning strategy? Of course not. Get in the gutter or go home.

Your mom told you to be nice, I know. But God bless her, this is terrible advice out there in the big, bad, real world. You can't afford to be nice. Right?

In 2003, Geoffrey Urbaniak and Peter Kilmann, two psychologists from the University of South Carolina, decided to study whether women really do choose jerks over nice guys, as everyone assumes.[1] They recruited forty-eight female volunteers at a small, northeastern liberal arts college and had them read the script to a mock version of the popular 1970s TV game show *The Dating Game*, in which a female contestant would quiz men hidden behind a screen and then choose one to date based solely on their answers. In the mock script, an imaginary contestant named Susan must choose between two men named (not coincidentally) Michael and Todd. Michael stays constant and neutral, while the participants were randomly assigned three different variations of Todd:

The first was Nice Todd, who is kind, attentive, and emotionally expressive. When asked what his definition is of a "real man," Nice Todd replies:

> A real man is someone who is in touch with his feelings and those of his partner. Someone who is kind and attentive and doesn't go for all that macho stuff. He's also great in the bedroom and puts his partner's pleasure first. I'd definitely say I'm a real man.

Second is Middle Todd, who gives neutral responses. He tells Susan:

> A real man knows what he wants and he knows how to get it. Someone who works hard and plays hard, and who is good to the woman he loves. He's also great in the bedroom. I'd definitely say I'm a real man.

Third is Jerk Todd, who is an insensitive, self-absorbed, macho jerk:

> A real man knows what he wants and he knows how to get it. Someone who knows who he is, but keeps other people guessing and on their toes—he doesn't go in for all that touchy-feely stuff. He's also great in the bedroom and can tell his partner what he likes. I'd definitely say I'm a real man.

In all the scenarios, Todd is competing against neutral Michael, who tells Susan:

> A real man is relaxed. He doesn't let the world get him down. He's confident, solid, and keeps a positive attitude at all times. He's also a great kisser—and I'm definitely one of those!

After reading the script, the participants were asked whether Susan should pick Todd or Michael. The result? Nice Todd was chosen over Michael 81 percent of the time, while Jerk Todd beat out Michael a mere 7 percent of the time. When asked for their own preferences, the women chose Nice Todd over Michael at a rate of almost 70 percent, and only a single individual selected Jerk Todd over Michael. Not only was Nice Todd chosen the most frequently of all options, participants also rated him as more intelligent and just as exciting as Jerk Todd (which undercuts the popular notion that women find nice guys less interesting or exciting than jerks). "The results provide support for the notion that women's preferences do match their behaviors and that nice guys are preferred," the authors write. "The nicer Todd was portrayed, the more often he was chosen and the more desirable he was rated across different relationship contexts."

So far so good. But in the study (as in *The Dating Game*) the women could not actually see Todd and Michael. The premise of the show was to force women to choose based on personality, not looks. But in real life, we all know that physical attraction matters. Urbaniak and Kilmann wanted to know: Would women choose an attractive jerk over an average-looking nice guy?

To find out, they decided to replicate their study, but this time they showed the women pictures of Todd and Michael. They varied Todd's levels of handsomeness as well as "niceness" while keeping Michael constant and neutral in both looks and personality. The results were clear and conclusive. When their looks were equivalent, Nice Todd outperformed Michael. But the most stunning result was that Jerk Todd lost 85 percent of the time to Michael *even when Todd was better looking*.

Michael was "overwhelmingly chosen despite his being less attractive than Todd," they found. "The majority of women rejected the insensitive man even when he was more physically attractive than his counterpart."

Ever wonder if there is evidence of the existence of God? Well, there you are. You're welcome.

So where does the stereotype come from of nice guys being less attractive to women? A 1999 study from two Canadian researchers, which looked at university-age women, found that "nice" is often a polite euphemism for "needy, weak, predictable, boring, inexperienced, and unattractive."[2] As in, "He's . . . *nice*." In contrast, when men really *are* simply nice people, women prefer them.

It's not only niceness that women find attractive. It turns out that being generous to the needy makes men seem more handsome. In 2009, Dutch and British researchers showed female college students one of three videos featuring the same actor. In the first, he gives generously to a beggar on the street; in the second, he hands over just a little money; and in the third, the man gives nothing. The more he gave, the more handsome he appeared to the women in the study.[3]

A few years later, psychologists in the United Kingdom found something similar. They showed women pictures of two different men (one very handsome, the other much less so) and asked about the desirability of those men under different scenarios. In one, the two men are walking through a busy town and notice a homeless man sitting outside of a café. One decides to go into the café and buy a sandwich and cup of tea for the homeless person, while the other pretends to be busy on a mobile phone and walks past him. Whether handsome or not, the men who acted altruistically were viewed as more desirable for long-term relationships. Indeed, highly altruistic but unattractive men were rated as more desirable than minimally altruistic but highly attractive men. With respect to short-term relationships, handsome, altruistic men were also most highly rated. (The study did find, however, that women rated handsome, non-altruistic men slightly more desirable for short-term relationships than unattractive but altruistic men. Jerks, it seems, can sometimes be good for a fling, but in the long run the nice guy gets the girl.)[4]

By the way, if I seem to be focusing only on men here, that's because this is where the research is. *Much* less is written about whether men prefer nice women. The few studies generally find that men do tend to prefer women who are friendly and nice—because they interpret that as an expression of sexual interest.[5] (At this point, I know, you're face-palming.)

Kindness goes a long way in the world of romance,

but what about at the office? In 2015, researchers at Georgetown University and the Grenoble School of Management conducted a workplace study that asked the question, "Being nice may bring you friends, but does it help or harm you in your career?"[6] To find out, they examined the effect of being nice and civil in the workplace on three specific work outcomes: (1) being sought out for advice; (2) being perceived as a leader; and (3) job performance.

Those who practiced kindness came out ahead in all three categories. When colleagues see a coworker as nice and civil, they will be "more likely to seek that person out for work advice and to see that person as a leader," the researchers found. Nice people were also seen by their colleagues as more competent, and they got better performance reviews from their supervisors. Indeed, the researchers found, they performed better precisely *because* they were nice. It turns out that being nice "increase[s] the likelihood that others seek—and presumably exchange—information and advice, which, in turn, increase[s] performance." If you want to be perceived as a future leader, be promoted, and get a raise, be nice to your coworkers.

The social science is clear: Nice guys in love, and nice people at work, do not finish last. Your mom was right after all. Of course.

What about leadership? For a long time, people sub-scribed to the notion that Jerk Todd could do just fine in political office or the corner office, as long as he was good-looking and smooth-talking—a politician or CEO from the movies, in other words. And in fact, lots of studies have shown that attractive extroverts are much preferred by the public for leadership positions.

Lately, however, our understanding of this has be-come more nuanced. In 2013, researchers in the journal *Psychological Science* showed that voters usually elect good-looking politicians, not because we are hopelessly shallow, but because this is a powerful brain cue that the person is healthy.[7] (People naturally want leaders who are unlikely to keel over, apparently.) This matches new work in brain science showing that physical attractive-ness provides intuitive cues to potential mates about their ability to have children or support a family.

However, positive personality traits also turn out to matter a lot when we pick leaders. Social psychologist Amy Cuddy has studied leader personalities a great deal and says, "The way to influence—and to lead—is to begin with warmth. Warmth is the conduit of influence: It facilitates trust and the communication and absorption of ideas."[8] She cites a survey of nearly fifty-two thousand leaders, sorted by likability and leadership effectiveness.

These data show that only 0.05 percent of leaders (one in two thousand) are in the bottom quartile for likability but the top quartile for leadership effectiveness. People do *not* want to follow jerks if they don't have to.

Similarly, the Georgetown/Grenoble study concluded, "Rather than hurting themselves by appearing weak or deferential, behaving respectfully seems to garner influence." The researchers found that "for leaders and potential leaders, civility appears to be very valuable—it elicits warmth, allowing for an initial connection or relationship to take root; yet it also signals the ability to lead."

But forget the data for a moment. Think about your own life. Which bosses have you had whom you liked and admired? I bet it wasn't the jerks. Now ask yourself which are the stories of leadership that inspire you. Are they about horrible people? More likely, they feature leaders lifted up by others because of their virtue and goodness, often against all odds. In their bestseller *The 5 Patterns of Extraordinary Careers*, business authors James M. Citrin and Richard A. Smith found that the greatest leaders are carried to their success by followers who love them.[9]

One of my favorite stories that makes this point in a world-historic way is that of Nelson Mandela. He was held for twenty-seven years as a political prisoner by a government that had institutionalized racial injustice.[10] He was subjected to grueling manual labor, breaking rocks each day. His sight was permanently damaged by the glare of the sun in the quarry in which he was made to work. He slept in a cell that was hardly as long as he was tall.

How did Mandela react to his persecutors? Many of us might have lashed out with contempt or shrunk away in despair. Instead, he befriended his captors, learning their language and treating them with warmth. He even took up an interest in their favorite sport—rugby. You might be tempted to say that Mandela suffered from Stockholm syndrome, hostages' tendency to sympathize with their captors; that the oppression and brutality had had their desired effect.

You'd be wrong. Mandela had a conviction that only goodness could win in a moral struggle. He believed that even under unjust persecution, people should treat others with kindness and respect, that anything less was a failing of his own character.

Of course, Mandela did not die in prison. He emerged in 1990 and led an end to apartheid while ushering in a new era of healing in South Africa. He threw himself into efforts to right the wrongs of the past decades, and did so in the same way he behaved in prison. He met with Betsie Verwoerd, the widow of apartheid's architect, Hendrik Verwoerd, in order to model rec-onciliation and kindness. Along with F. W. de Klerk, South Africa's president, Mandela was awarded a Nobel Peace Prize in 1993 for his work in bringing about peaceful, democratic change. He was elected president of South Africa in 1994, signaling a massive victory for the cause of national solidarity. And in a profound act of national unity, Mandela encouraged all South Africans to cheer for the country's rugby team in the 1995 World Cup. Under the banner of "One Team, One Nation," South Africa's underdog Springboks—once a notorious symbol of the country's racial divisions—took home the crown.

Deservedly, Mandela is remembered as one of history's greatest leaders. His greatness owes to his strength and courage, to be sure, but also to the goodness he displayed to everyone, including his captors. In modern life, we are often taught that we have to choose between kindness and success; Mandela showed that this is not a choice we have to make. On the contrary, we can learn from his style of cheerful, kind leadership while striking a blow against the culture of contempt.

So why are there so many Jerk Todds today in politics, business, and media? It doesn't really make sense in efficient markets like these. There is an answer to that question, as you will see in the next chapter. In the meantime, however, the key takeaway for you is this: Whether you are a politician, a CEO, or just an ordinary citizen intent on changing the country, you *can* afford to be nice. In fact, you can hardly afford *not* to be nice.

How does one be nice? My glib answer is that if you have to ask, you're really in trouble. That's too facile, though, because it isn't always clear in today's world. Much of the time, we feel under siege and have little niceness in our hearts. Given the vitriol we experience, to be truly nice probably requires years of meditation and intense study. If you're up for that, great! But that's a long-term solution. Want a couple of hacks instead?

Here's the first one: fake it. Even if you don't feel like being nice, act the way a nice person would. Soon enough, you'll actually become a nicer person and reap the rewards.

This seems counterintuitive. Most of us assume that our actions follow our emotions. If we feel happy, we act happy. If we feel joy, we smile. Action follows attitude. This is true in some cases, but it's only half the story. Ancient wisdom has always taught that attitude also follows action. In the words of Vietnamese Buddhist master Thich Nhat Hanh, "Sometimes your joy is the source of your smile, but sometimes your smile can be the source of your joy."[11]

Recent scientific work shows that this is true. This is the conclusion of "self-perception theory," which holds that acting "as if" one feels something will actually result in that feeling. One of the pioneers of this work is James Laird, a psychologist at Clark University in Worcester, Massachusetts. In 1974, he conducted a series of tests in which he induced subjects to force themselves to smile or frown. So that they didn't know what his purpose was, he attached fake electrodes to their faces and told them he was testing "the activity of facial muscles under various conditions." He then showed the test subjects pictures of children playing and Ku Klux Klan members marching, while they held a frown or a smile. Afterward, he had them take a test to measure their moods. He found that the participants "described themselves as happier when they were in a smile expression and angrier when they were in a frown expression," no matter the image they were viewing.

In a second experiment, Laird used the same setup but this time showed participants cartoons, while once again forcing them to either smile or frown. The subjects found "cartoons viewed while they were smiling to be more humorous than cartoons viewed while they were frowning." Laird concluded that "manipulation of the expressive behavior of the face was sufficient to produce changes in reports of subjective experience of emotion."[12]

The smile is a powerful weapon for leaders who seek to spread positivity and unify others. Indeed, a smile is so powerful, it can lower racial bias. In 2006, a team of researchers had seventy-three test subjects hold a smile while viewing photographs of unfamiliar black or white males. Afterward, the researchers had the participants take an implicit-association test (IAT), which measures racial bias. They found "significantly less racial bias against blacks among participants surreptitiously induced to smile during prior viewing of black faces than among participants surreptitiously induced to smile during prior viewing of white faces."[13] Turns out it's hard to hate when you have a smile on your face.

Why does smiling—whether spontaneous or by choice—make us happier and nicer? Because the act of smiling actually stimulates the part of the brain that's associated with positive emotions. In 1993, psychologists Paul Ekman and Richard Davidson asked a group of undergraduates to hold nine different facial expressions for twenty seconds each while they ran an electroencephalogram (EEG) to measure electrical activity in the brain.[14] They found that both manipulated and spontaneous smiles resulted in the same physiological effect—you can actually choose to activate the happiness centers of your brain by forcing yourself to smile.

These and other findings have revolutionized the way many therapists treat depression and other psychological disorders. In addition to antidepressants, many psychologists and psychiatrists now also recommend cognitive behavioral therapy for their patients—a form of psychotherapy that boosts happiness by modifying dysfunctional attitudes and behaviors. It turns out that when people are unhappy, they tend to behave in certain ways. They become physically immobile, stay in bed, frown a lot, and interact infrequently with other people. Conversely, there are certain things that happy people do. They get up and move around, get out of the house, engage with other people—and smile. In cognitive behavioral therapy, one of the things psychologists tell their depressed patients is to try to act the way happy people do. Instead of staying in your pajamas all day, get out of bed, take a shower, get dressed, eat your breakfast, go outside, and talk to people. Even if you feel miserable, smile and pretend you're happy. Your emotions will conform to your actions, at least somewhat.

The reverse is also true. If you start acting like a depressed person, you're going to start feeling depressed. This is something every parent intuitively understands. If your kids start hanging around other kids who are wearing black, acting bummed out, and engaging in self-destructive behaviors, your kids are going to start feeling more depressed. By contrast, if your kids hang out with happy kids who go outside, run around, smile and laugh, and play sports, they are going to be happier. There's a reason that moms say to their kids, "It's a beautiful day! Get out of the house!" (When I was a kid, moms would ban their kids from the house. But those were different times.) Going out is what happy people do. They get out of the house and enjoy the beautiful weather. Moms want their kids to be happy, and they intuitively know that attitude follows action.

This knowledge can save marriages. In his bestselling classic, *The 7 Habits of Highly Effective People*, Stephen Covey recounts how a man came to one of his seminars and told him, "Look at my marriage. I'm really worried. My wife and I just don't have the same feelings for each other we used to have. I guess I just don't love her anymore and she doesn't love me. What can I do?"[15] Covey told him the answer was simple. He should love her. But, the man protested, he didn't *feel* love anymore. "How do you love when you don't love?" the man asked.

"My friend," Covey replied, "love is a verb. Love—the feeling—is a fruit of love, the verb. So love her. Serve her. Sacrifice. Listen to her. Empathize. Appreciate.

Affirm her." If he did those things, if he treated her with love, Covey promised, he would feel love for her again, because feelings follow action. "If our feelings control our actions, it is because we have abdicated our responsibility and empowered them to do so," Covey writes. "Reactive people make [love] a feeling. . . . Proactive people make love a verb. Love is something you do: the sacrifices you make, the giving of self. . . . Love is a value that is actualized through loving actions. Proactive people subordinate feelings to values. Love, the feeling, can be recaptured."

(By the way, go read Covey's book. You may have thought it's just cheesy self-help, but it is actually a masterpiece. In many ways, it changed my life for the better.)

For more than fifty years, husband-and-wife social psychologists Arthur and Elaine Aron have been studying how people fall in love. In 1997, they conducted a study to see if "interpersonal closeness"—whether friendship or romantic love—could be generated between two complete strangers in a laboratory in just forty-five minutes.[16] They brought together men and women who did not know each other, sat them down face-to-face in a lab, and had them ask each other a series of thirty-six increasingly intimate questions. After they were done with the questions, they had the men and women gaze into each other's eyes for four minutes.[17] The result? "At the end of 45 minutes, you feel as close to this person, almost as the closest person in your life," Arthur Aron says.[18] Indeed, one couple in the study became so close, they ended up getting married.

What does all this mean for you? Act like the person you want to be—one who is nice to others, decent, warm, and happy. Don't feel it? Fake it. Pretend you have an innate sense of brotherhood and solidarity even if you don't. Act like a uniter even if you don't feel like one. Eventually your attitude will follow your actions.

We don't have to feel unity and brotherhood. We simply need to *act* in a spirit of unity and brotherhood, and the feelings will follow. By the same token, if we allow ourselves to indulge in habits of contempt—frowning as we listen to talk radio or getting angry at the latest outrageous statement from a politician—our emotions will follow those actions as well. One of Dr. Laird's test subjects, who was forced to frown during an experiment, told him, "When my jaw was clenched and my brows down, I tried not to be angry but it just fit the position. I'm not in any angry mood but I found my thoughts wandering to things that made me angry, which is sort of silly, I guess. I knew I was in an experiment and knew

I had no reason to feel that way, but I just lost control." He might as well have been describing what happens when most people watch cable TV news today.

If you think this makes you into some kind of a fake, you are exactly wrong. This puts you in control, where you belong. Do you want to be the kind of person who is tossed from emotion to emotion and reacts to others according to your current mood? Or do you want to be a leader to yourself? If the latter, then act like the leader, and take control of your outward appearance.

Hack number two for becoming nicer and happier is also simple: show gratitude. Gratitude is, quite simply, a contempt killer. You cannot have contempt for someone to whom you are grateful. And guess what? Just as you can make yourself smile, you can also make yourself grateful—even if you don't feel it.

It's like a magic trick, and indeed, it was a famous magician who showed people how to perform that trick. In the 1930s, the self-improvement pioneer Dale Carnegie published his world-renowned bestseller *How to Win Friends and Influence People*. It has sold more than thirty million copies since it was first published eighty years ago.

(By the way, like Covey's, this is also a beautiful book. The title sounds like a how-to guide for bending people to your will, but it's actually a guide to courageous, ethical living and treating others with respect.)

When he was researching the book, Carnegie traveled across America to find the most successful people and uncover their secrets. When he got to New York City, he went to Broadway to see the last performance of the most famous magician of his age: Howard Thurston.[19]

Thurston had come from nothing. "He ran away from home as a small boy, became a hobo, rode in boxcars, slept in haystacks, begged his food from door to door, and learned to read by looking out of boxcars at signs along the railway," Carnegie writes. Yet from these humble origins, he rose to become one of the biggest performers of his time. His traveling magic show needed eight train cars to transport his equipment. "For forty years he had traveled all over the world, time and again, creating illusions, mystifying audiences, and making people gasp with astonishment," Carnegie says. He performed before more than sixty million people—almost unheard of in the age before television—and earned almost $2 million (the equivalent of about $23 million in today's dollars).

Dale Carnegie visited Thurston's dressing room after his last show and asked him the secret of his success. Was there something special about the tricks he performed? No, Thurston told him, his tricks were fairly conventional—nothing you could not find in magic books.

The true secret of his success, Thurston told him, was *gratitude*. "He told me that many magicians would look at the audience and say to themselves, 'Well, there is a bunch of suckers out there, a bunch of hicks; I'll fool them all right,'" Carnegie writes. "But Thurston's method was totally different. He told me that every time he went onstage he said to himself: 'I am grateful because these people come to see me. They make it possible for me to make my living in a very agreeable way. I'm going to give them the very best I possibly can.' He declared he never stepped in front of the footlights without first saying to himself over and over: 'I love my audience. I love my audience.'" (I'll bet he smiled while saying it.)

Howard Thurston knew intuitively what scientists have since proved: the key to being nicer and happier is gratitude. In one 2003 study, researchers asked undergraduate students to write a report of their experiences once a week for a ten-week period.[20] One group was asked to list "five things in your life that you are grateful or thankful for." A second group was asked to list each week "five hassles that occurred in your life." A third was asked to simply list "five events that had an impact on you," whether good or bad.

The study found that people who kept a list of things

they were grateful for were significantly more satisfied with their lives than subjects who dwelled on negative or neutral events instead. "Participants in the gratitude condition felt better about their lives as a whole, and were more optimistic regarding their expectations for the upcoming week," they found. "They reported fewer physical complaints and reported spending significantly more time exercising."

When the researchers raised the stakes and asked participants to keep a daily gratitude journal for two weeks, they found the participants not only were happier, but "they were also more likely to report having helped someone with a personal problem or offered emotional support to another." When they were asked to keep a daily gratitude journal for three weeks, researchers found it also "improved people's amount of sleep and the quality of that sleep" and that "the effects on well-being (positive affect and life satisfaction) were apparent to the participants' spouse or significant other."

The lesson is clear: to be happier and to be better to others, count your blessings.

You may object that sometimes it's hard to feel gratitude, especially when we face people who treat us with hostility or contempt. This is exactly when we need gratitude the most, and this difficulty gets to the very heart of what this book is about. In Luke's Gospel, Jesus warns, "If you love those who love you, what credit is that to you? For even sinners love those who love them. . . . But love your enemies. . . . Then your reward will be great."[21] Or take the words of Abraham Lincoln in his First Inaugural Address, "We are not enemies, but friends. We must not be enemies. Though passion may have strained, it must not break our bonds of affection."[22]

As a person with center-right views who speaks on college campuses, I face difficult audiences all the time. I have faculty and students who come to my speeches expecting me to say reactionary things and ready to fight me. As I walk onstage, I see lots of frowns and folded arms. I won't lie to you . . . it is stressful to face big groups who judge you before you even say a word. Each time, I try to channel my inner Howard Thurston and say to myself before I go onstage, "I love my audience, and I am grateful they showed up to listen to me. I need them."

For me, the last part is key to national unity: gratitude based on a recognition that we need others, even—perhaps especially—those with whom we disagree. Why? Because we are blessed to live in the greatest, freest country in the history of the world—a place where, when you have a difference of opinion, nobody's going to knock on your door and haul you off to a forced-labor camp. We take this for granted, but in the scope of history, it is truly a miracle. If you join me in being grateful that we don't live in a one-party state, then by definition you must be grateful for people who disagree with you. They are the ones who make pluralism and democracy possible. You should be grateful and express that gratitude for people who are on the other side in the competition of ideas.

And if you don't feel it? You know what I'm going to say: act grateful anyway. Forget about your feelings and decide to count your blessings. Not only will doing so make you a happier person; it will make you more grateful—and bring us one step closer to defeating the culture of contempt.

A politician once told me that he felt a lot of anguish because he often had to be a person he didn't admire in order to win. He had to say things that were harsh and unkind, even though he wanted to be friendly and respectful. He was a conservative, but felt backed into a corner by activists on his own side who would accuse him of being a "cuckservative" (a cuckolded or emasculated conservative) or a "beta" (as opposed to an alpha male). I understood his conundrum, particularly in the current environment. Still, I flatly reject the premise that to win, one must be a jerk. There is no inconsistency between kindness and effective, winning leadership. This does not make me an idealist; it means I am paying attention to the best evidence. Indeed, it's the jerks who sooner or later wind up as the betas.

Is being nice difficult? Sure—it requires skill and practice, like anything else that's worthwhile. But it is not impossible. This chapter has laid out the principles to leadership that aims at both virtue and victory, a kind of leadership modeled by the likes of Mandela, Lincoln, and the Dalai Lama. It starts with a commitment to acting the way you want to be, not the way you feel at any given moment. With some smiling, gratitude, and repetition, you can and will become a nicer person, a leader admired by others, and a greater force for good.

Chapter 3
Love Lessons for Leaders

In the late 1980s and early 1990s, I was the associate principal French hornist with the City Orchestra of Barcelona, Spain. In hundreds of concerts, I performed the most exquisite symphonic works ever written, by some of the greatest musical geniuses in history: Mozart, Schubert, Beethoven, Brahms.

I hated it.

The problem wasn't the music. I love classical music, and have all my life. As a kid, my mother (a professional painter and amateur violinist) always had the classics playing in our home. She taught me about the composers' lives, and I learned to distinguish the subtleties of their compositional styles. I took up the violin at age four, the piano at five, and the French horn at nine. I knew by ten I would be a professional horn player, and I spent my entire youth doing little else but practicing, studying, competing, and performing. On my bedroom wall, I had pictures of famous French horn players for inspiration.

Unable to stand the idea of four years of college, I left after just one and started my professional career, playing chamber music. At twenty-five, I got the job in Barcelona. I thrilled at the prospect of playing the orchestral pieces I had heard since my youth.

So why did it turn out to be unpleasant? Simple: the conductors. They were notorious bullies, cruel and demanding, with near-total control over the artistic lives of the players. To consolidate power, they turned players against one another, preyed on weakness, destroyed confidence. As we used to note, some conductors are evil geniuses, but *all are evil.**

The French horn is an especially perilous job in an orchestra, exposed and prone for reasons of physics to miss notes. This opens the player to a conductor's scorn and mockery. Once, after missing a note in a devilishly hard solo during a rehearsal, the conductor stopped the orchestra, looked at me with contempt, and said,

---

* My position on conductors has softened since those days. Some, I have learned, are wonderful people. This attitude shift coincides with my own move into management, so take it as you will.

"Mr. Brooks, please stop making mistakes." In my head, I plotted his murder.

If it was so bad, why didn't we rise up as one? Why didn't we strike or rebel in some other way? Because deep down, a lot of the players believed that a tyrant was what we needed. At one point during my tenure in Barcelona, we were in the market for a new conductor. The old guy was a bully, but the leading contender for his job took it up a notch. I had seen him reduce a sixty-five-year-old man in the flute section to tears. In his patent-leather shoes I'm pretty sure I would have found cloven hoofs.

I was discussing him with the horn player next to me, a Spaniard. "What a disaster it'll be if the administration picks this guy as the new maestro," I commented.

"Yeah, he's terrible," my companion answered. "But he's the right choice. A Spanish orchestra needs a tyrant."

That, in a nutshell, is the paradox of contemptuous leaders. We may not like them, but we sometimes feel like we need them. Like when? Maybe right about now, in America. Our country has become a Spanish orchestra—fractious, undisciplined, practically ungovernable. Many Americans intuitively see things the way my colleague in Barcelona did. We have big problems, and the times require tough leaders. If we want a better orchestra, we don't need kindness, happiness, and gratitude. We need leaders who are willing to break a few eggs, and maybe even a few heads. Right?

If we're going to discuss leadership, we need to start with one hard truth: tyrannical or not, people don't enjoy being around leaders all that much. One study from Nobel laureate Daniel Kahneman and his colleagues looked at sources of unhappiness in our ordinary lives.[1] They found that, on average, our bosses at work are the number one unhappiness-provoking individuals with whom we spend time on any given day. Leaders who think their employees look forward to seeing them are basically fooling themselves. (As a boss, I think I might just have lunch at my desk from now on.) Most leaders want to be the exception; few are. Why? Because most people find it stressful to be bossed.

In truth, most of us in leadership roles have made an uneasy peace with this truth. Tyrants, on the other hand, embrace it fully. The canonical text for despotic leaders is Niccolò Machiavelli's classic *The Prince*, in which he famously advised, "It is much safer to be feared than loved, if one has to lack one of the two."[2] By process of elimination, since you cannot be loved and still be the boss, go ahead and be fully feared.

People who follow this advice are what psychologist Daniel Goleman calls "coercive leaders" in his seminal *Harvard Business Review* article "Leadership That Gets Results."[3] In his research, he studied the leadership styles of nearly four thousand CEOs. The most hated? "Coercive leadership." The coercive leader, Goleman writes, creates "a reign of terror, bullying and demeaning his executives, roaring his displeasure at the slightest misstep."

Man, that's the maestro described to a T. And it sounds like a lot of current leaders in our political discourse. From television to social media to everyday politics at the highest level, we see powerful people belittling, maligning, and mocking those with lower status. Citizens, colleagues, and opponents are all routinely insulted and shamed in a system that rewards the loudest voices and most audacious claims.

Is this what we really want? I couldn't pick my conductors; they were imposed on me by the orchestra management (or perhaps by Satan himself, I'm not sure). I never voted for any of them. We *vote* for our politicians. And lately, we *select* coercive leaders. Why?

Dr. Goleman provides an answer that sounds like that of my colleague in the Spanish orchestra. Imagine that you were working at a company that had been horribly mismanaged by leaders who had brought the business to the brink of bankruptcy. You might welcome the arrival of a coercive leader ready to shake up the system. Goleman describes one such executive who was brought in to save a food company that was losing money. "His first act was to have the executive conference room demolished. To him, the room—with its long marble table that looked like 'the deck of the Starship Enterprise'—symbolized the tradition-bound formality that was paralyzing the company." The demolition was cheered by the rank and file, because it sent a message that the failing culture had to change.

Likewise, divisive, coercive political leaders can be appealing during times of national despair, when voters want to change the status quo. If people are convinced that a crisis is being ignored, a coercive leader might be just what they want, at least for a little while. Sound familiar? Maybe like the story of our political moment? No matter what your political views, Goleman's model helps you understand how we got to our current state of contemptuous politics. Let's do a walk-through, step by step.

In the decade before the 2016 presidential election, Americans had been through an economic crisis worse than anything since the Great Depression of the 1930s. Millions lost their homes or jobs or both. Huge swaths of people felt left behind by the economic recovery and forgotten by the political classes in Washington, who were offering them no solutions and didn't seem to care much about their plight.

Their despair didn't register in public opinion surveys. Neither the conventional left nor the conventional right fully grasped it. For decades, conventional conservatives had emphasized issues such as entitlement reform, which is important for the solvency of the country but feels cold and remote to voters worried about losing their job and benefits. Meanwhile, the conventional political left focused on the "income gap" separating rich and poor. They contended that income inequality would ignite a new class struggle, causing unprecedented political turmoil. This was half right. There was indeed a gap in this country, but the relevant gap wasn't income. It was dignity.

We sense dignity by creating value with our lives, through families, communities, and especially work. That is why American leaders so frequently talk about dignity in the context of work. As Martin Luther King Jr. taught, "All labor that uplifts humanity has dignity and importance and should be undertaken with painstaking excellence."[4] Conversely, nothing destroys dignity more than idleness and a sense of superfluousness—the feeling that one is simply not needed.

That is the circumstance in which millions of

Americans found themselves as the 2016 election approached. Bestselling books over the past few years, such as Charles Murray's *Coming Apart*, Robert Putnam's *Our Kids*, and J. D. Vance's *Hillbilly Elegy* tell the story. Even with strong economic growth, the United States has bifurcated into a nation of socioeconomic winners and losers, and this stratification is poisoning American culture. As the future fills with whiz-bang technologies, from artificial intelligence to driverless cars, one part of the population sees ingenuity, mobility, and progress. Another part hears, "We don't need you anymore." This is the *dignity gap.*

Who falls on the wrong side of this dignity gap? Lots of people of all races and classes, but to an especially large extent, it is working-class men. In his recent book, *Men Without Work*, political economist and demographer Nicholas Eberstadt shows that the percentage of working-age men outside the labor force—that is, neither working nor seeking work—has more than tripled since 1965, rising from 3.4 percent to 11.5 percent.[5] And men without a high school diploma are more than twice as likely to be part of this "nonworking class."[6]

This retreat from the labor force was amplified by the sluggish recovery that most Americans experienced after the Great Recession. Only about the top fifth of the economy saw positive income growth for most of the Obama presidency, Census Bureau data show, while most others averaged no growth at all. This stagnation devastated men without a college education, especially in rural areas.

These men have withdrawn not only from the labor force but from other social institutions as well. Eberstadt found that, despite their lack of work obligations, men without work are no more likely to spend time volunteering, participating in religious activities, or caring for family members than men with full-time employment.[7] Almost half of them are unmarried.

Life without dignity can produce shocking results. Social isolation and idleness correlate with severe pathologies, as in the rural areas where drug abuse and suicide have become far more common in recent years. In 2015, Princeton economists Anne Case and Angus Deaton published an extraordinary paper in the *Proceedings of the National Academy of Sciences*.[8] They found that, in contrast to the favorable long-term trends in life expectancy across most of the population, the mortality rate among middle-aged white Americans with no college education has actually risen since 1999. They are the only demographic group for whom this is true. The main reasons? Cirrhosis of the liver (up 50 percent since 1999 among this group), suicide (up 78 percent), and drug overdoses, primarily of opiates (up 323 percent).

Do these data amaze you? According to the National Institute on Drug Abuse, about 72,000 Americans died from drug overdoses in 2017.[9] We are in the midst of the worst OD disaster in American history, by far. At the peak of the heroin epidemic of 1973–75, there were 1.5 opioid fatalities per 100,000 members of the population.[10] In 2017, it was 15 per 100,000. In the 1970s, there was a national panic about drugs, and everyone knew someone who had gotten addicted. Yet today, with ten times the death toll as a percentage of the population, an informed person who cares about others and loves this country might very well know no one who has a drug problem at all. This is further evidence of how we are coming apart, how a country in crisis can have leadership that is effectively in the dark about these deaths of despair and America's dignity gap.

Two Americas, two views of the future. As wealth levels soar and overall economic growth is solid, those on the wrong side of the dignity gap hold a distinctly gloomy outlook. For example, according to a survey conducted in 2016 by the Kaiser Family Foundation and CNN, fewer than one-quarter of white Americans without a college degree expect their children to enjoy a better standard of living in the future than they themselves have today, and half of them believe things will be even worse.[11] In contrast, according to the same survey, some historically marginalized communities enjoy more optimism: 36 percent of working-class African Americans and 48 percent of working-class Hispanics anticipate a better life for their children.

To be sure, working-class men with few in-demand skills and little education are hardly the only vulnerable group in the United States today. But the evidence is undeniable that this community is suffering an acute dignity crisis.

At its core, to be treated with dignity means being considered worthy of respect. Certain situations bring out a clear, conscious sense of our own dignity: when we receive praise or promotions at work, when we see our children succeed, or when we see a volunteer effort pay off and change our neighborhood for the better. We feel a sense of dignity when our own lives produce value for ourselves and others.

Put simply, to feel dignified, one must be needed by others. Millions of Americans no longer feel needed—by their families, their communities, the economy, or their country. Left behind every bit as much as the urban poor, millions of working-class men languished for years while people in power ignored them or treated them with contempt.

Many of these Americans didn't bother voting in the past. Others threw their lot in with traditional politicians. Most were ready for outsiders who promised to blow up the old ways of doing business.

Then, in 2016, two men burst onto the scene who were ready to do just that: Donald Trump and Bernie Sanders—political entrepreneurs who recognized that these voters were expressing a demand for leadership that the political establishments of both parties didn't meet. So when they threw their hats into the ring, both of their campaigns caught fire—because they tapped into that latent demand for dignity among all forgotten Americans. Their coercive, throw-out-the-playbook leadership styles were not a disadvantage; they made all the difference.

It was only because the Democratic primary process was less open than the GOP's that Sanders did not win the Democratic nomination, while Trump won the Republican nomination. As a result, these Americans were left with a choice in 2016 between conventional Democrat Hillary Clinton and unconventional Republican Donald Trump. Millions didn't hesitate to embrace the unconventional outsider who promised to fight for them.

Despite their vastly different personalities, Trump and Sanders were actually viewed by many voters as practically interchangeable. As amazing as it might seem to partisan Democrats and Republicans, I spoke to many people who said they would vote for either Trump or

Sanders, but no one else. On Election Day, about 12 percent of Bernie Sanders supporters in the Democratic primary voted for Donald Trump in the general election.[12] These Sanders voters gave Trump the margin of victory in Wisconsin, Michigan, and Pennsylvania—the three states that in the end handed Trump the White House.[13] You read that right: One reason Donald Trump is president of the United States as I write these words is because of Bernie Sanders's supporters.

Many people from all walks of life voted for Donald Trump, but the demographic core of his support matches the vulnerable group that Eberstadt, Case, and Deaton identify. Exit polls show Trump beat Hillary Clinton among white men without a college degree by nearly *50 percentage points*.[14] He did so without forsaking the limited support that Mitt Romney received from African American and Hispanic men.[15] Tellingly, among counties where Trump outperformed Romney four years earlier, the margins were greatest in those places with the highest rates of illegal drug use, alcohol abuse, and suicide.[16] He successfully stimulated voters who had not voted in a very long time or had done so in a disinterested way. These new voters were key to flipping the nearly 220 counties that went blue in 2012 but landed in Trump's column on Election Day 2016.[17]

Trump won these voters because he saw a crisis of

dignity that was unmet by conventional politicians. These voters wanted a leader who would shake up the system. They wanted someone who, like Goleman's food executive, would smash the marble conference table around which the elites gathered, and force a new political reality.

A crisis explains the emergence of coercive leaders, in business and politics. As Goleman notes, they can be appealing and even somewhat effective in the short run, if for no other reason than that, at least in appearance, they put an abrupt end to what people consider an unacceptable status quo. For an organization in free fall, this is not a small victory. In the long run, however, coercive leaders are not what people want, so coercive leadership often ends badly, in scandal or ignominious defeat.

Even after they have finished their term of short-lived usefulness, though, coercive leaders can persist for some time. First, the polarization they feed on in a company or country can keep them in power. The other side's political bully is a horrible person; your side's bully is a truth-teller. Indeed, we sometimes even flip the script and say our bully is actually the *victim*, and simply fighting back against even bigger bullies. That is certainly the case in American politics and media today.

I constantly hear people complain about their own side's leaders and pundits, only to say that the other side is so much worse that we need people willing to fight dirty.

Second, coercive leaders can hang on because few people want to be the one who stands up to them with no assurance that there will be popular support. A coercive leader is kind of like an abusive drunk on the subway. He can hold the whole car hostage because no one wants to be the object of his threatened violence. The objective for thirty people can be to avoid his gaze until it's time to get off the train.

This is a well-documented behavioral phenomenon. In a famous 1999 article in the *Journal of Adolescence*, three psychologists asked how children typically act when they witness an instance of bullying.[18] Hundreds of schoolchildren were videotaped on the playground, and nearly two hundred bullying incidents were recorded. Bullies love audiences, and in more than half of the cases, two or more peers were present in addition to the bully and victim. How did the peers react? Twenty-one percent joined the bully, while 25 percent defended the victim. The rest—54 percent—watched the incident passively, neither joining in nor defending the victim.

Third, some people are paradoxically attracted to bullies. In her book *The Allure of Toxic Leaders*,

Claremont Graduate University professor Jean Lipman-Blumen shows that people complain about political dictators and tyrannical executives, yet nearly always remain loyal out of a primordial admiration for power and a need for security in an uncertain world.[19]

In the orchestra, there is a joke that makes this last point. A viola player for years is singled out for abuse and torment by the conductor. One day, he comes home from rehearsal to find his house burned to the ground. The police on the scene tell him it's arson, and that there is evidence that the culprit is none other than the conductor himself. Asked if he has any questions, the violist thinks for a moment and asks softly, "The maestro came to my house?"

Coercive leaders can persist for a long time. Sooner or later, however, they fail. Coercive behavior destroys morale and leaves people alienated. As psychologists Jennifer Lerner and Larissa Tiedens note, tendencies toward blame and anger exhibited by coercive leaders escalate "in a recursive loop" and have "especially deleterious effects in interpersonal and intergroup relations."[20] People turn on one another and don't trust their colleagues or neighbors. Such leaders destroy trust and morale even among those who are not the direct objects of their coercive contempt.

Think about any dictatorship you've ever seen and

you'll understand the idea. Tyrants scapegoat and vilify others in order to maintain power. If you don't reject this as a follower, you imply assent. That creates in-groups and out-groups, which destroys trust and foments animosity. This certainly characterizes the current political moment in America, where one in six have ruptured a relationship over politics, doesn't it?

Beyond ruining relationships, coercive leadership also begets mediocrity. "The [coercive] leader's extreme top-down decision-making kills new ideas on the vine," Goleman writes. "People feel so disrespected that they think, 'I won't even bring my ideas up.'" No one tells the boss bad news for fear of getting blamed. Any sense of responsibility for the common good of the enterprise evaporates and is replaced by a culture of contempt. "Some become so resentful, they adopt the attitude, 'I'm not going to help this bastard.'"

Case in point: I remember one time in the middle of a concert when the conductor lost his place in the score. Not one of the eighty-five of us helped him (including my companion who thought he was a necessary evil). We preferred a bad performance to helping that guy. Later, we celebrated. This was an example of the dysfunction that led to his dismissal after just two years. Coercive leaders can bring out the worst, most self-destructive qualities in their followers.

Coercive leaders come at a high cost: cruelty, chaos, and a culture of contempt. They may produce short-term wins, and may hang on for some time, but people ultimately become tired of the collateral damage they cause. Constant conflict is exhausting, drives away excellence, and destroys morale. People don't like to be belittled by the leader or see others humiliated. Moreover, when the competition of ideas within a business or government is shut down, the long-term impact can be ruinous.

That describes our political moment today. At present, the coercive-leadership model appears to be proliferating in Washington, as both parties are paralyzed by division and contempt. It has also spread through the media, much of which specializes in caricatures of one side or the other. And many college campuses today are struggling to maintain the standards of free speech and idea diversity on which they were founded.

Divisive leaders on the left preach the politics of envy, while divisive leaders on the right promote the politics of exclusion. As mutual contempt rises, people increasingly refuse to work together. They become so resentful, they adopt the attitude, "I'm not going to help this bastard." Instead of having productive policy debates, they start trying to shut down the competition of ideas by attacking the other side as immoral and unworthy of participating in any civilized national discussion. The goal becomes not to help struggling Americans but to destroy the other side.

Can a new generation of leaders who want a better country address the needs for dignity and opportunity without the costs of coercive leadership? The answer is yes, and it takes us back once again to Goleman's research on leaders. Specifically, we need what he calls *authoritative leadership*. In his data analysis, he finds that these are far and away the most effective leaders for long-lasting prosperity and success.

Authoritative leaders in a company, according to Goleman, are visionaries who set a course for an institution and inspire each member to take responsibility for getting to the final destination. While coercive leaders drive people away by belittling and blaming, authoritative leaders garner their support by offering their encouragement and trust. They foster a culture that affirms each team member's importance to the work being done, and in doing so, convince individuals to invest deeply in the long-term prosperity of the organization. The aspirational approach of authoritative leaders produces the kind of success that builds on itself over time.

While authoritative leaders promote their own overarching vision, they are not *authoritarian*. They do not suppress dissent, instead granting employees the free-dom to disagree and solve problems on their own. The operational freedom granted by authoritative leaders promotes the individual creativity, accountability, and initiative that is essential to the success of any business.

Authoritative leaders inspire a can-do spirit and en-thusiasm for an organization's work because they ensure that no one feels muzzled or left behind. By letting every person know how her role helps accomplish the organization's mission, an authoritative leader empow-ers and motivates employees to become creative problem solvers.

Goleman relates the story of a leader who turned around a floundering pizza chain. While most of the company's executives were focused on preventing continued declines in sales, the leader in question was busy envisioning a new and better future. He defined a clear and simple vision—to distribute high-quality, convenient-to-get pizza to customers—and set local managers loose to figure out how to fulfill that mis-sion. Success followed in mere weeks as managers began guaranteeing faster delivery times and finding oppor-tune locations at which to open new branches—all with-out a harsh word.

Authoritative leadership is not advantageous only in business. It can be used in any setting, including

America's public life. Indeed, it is exactly what America's political discourse needs today.

If our goal is to restore dignity, it's not enough to smash a conference table or two and excoriate "the establishment." What we truly require is a *new vision* from authoritative leaders for the purpose of our economy and public policy. By articulating a clear aim of restoring human dignity and expanding opportunity, authoritative leaders can create space for Americans to think about old problems in new ways. Under the banner of such a vision, every American will be free to find better ways not just to "help" those who have been left behind, but to actually make them more *necessary*—more needed in their families, their communities, and the nation.

Authoritative leaders are not peacemakers. They aren't conflict-averse. They just understand how to manage conflict in a way that is not destructive.

Authoritative leaders know we need conflict in order to produce the best policies to help the chronically unemployed—the millions of Americans who, after years of trying, have given up on finding a job and dropped out of the labor force—find dignified work once again. They know we need disagreement about the best ways to reform the social safety net to increase incentives to seek employment without crushing those who need assistance or their families. They know we need competing ideas on how to rescue the millions of Americans addicted to drugs and hopeless about their futures. They know we need different approaches to help people become more necessary through better education, including ways to expand career- and technical-training programs, for the young and also middle-aged populations.

Sometimes this disagreement leads to a conflict of values. For authoritative leaders, that's all right, too. Their goal is not that we all just get along. In fact, they typically instigate vigorous debates and challenge people in uncomfortable ways. Jesus, the ultimate authoritative leader, said, "Do not suppose that I have come to bring peace to the earth. I did not come to bring peace, but a sword."[21] He turned over the money changers' tables in the temple.

In fact, authoritative leaders are capable of showing anger—but the right kind of anger. Anger comes in two major forms: That on one's own behalf and that on behalf of others. Coercive leaders often get angry on their own behalf. When somebody offends them, they get angry and lose control. Their anger is an expression of pride—and pride is perceived by others as weak and selfish. Prideful anger is the opposite of strength.

Authoritative leaders, by contrast, get angry on behalf of others, especially those who have no voice. That is called righteous anger, and within reason, it is a good and noble thing. It stimulates admiration. If you feel that politicians in Washington are hurting the poor or putting our national interest at risk, an authoritative leader can justifiably be angry. Righteous anger can motivate action and bring about positive social and political change. Nelson Mandela felt righteous anger over the injustice of apartheid and led the movement that peacefully ended white apartheid rule and ushered in a multiracial democracy.

Mandela also befriended the white prison guards who kept watch over him on Robben Island, which brings up another important point. The righteous anger of an authoritative leader doesn't cast anyone into outer darkness. It always promises to be forgotten when things are set right, because authoritative leaders have no permanent enemies and are capable of love for all. Authoritative leaders can get angry, but they are still nice people.

Righteous anger is an expression of generosity. It is kind to stand up for the oppressed. It is compassionate to fight for those who are weaker than you are. This kind of generosity is not weakness. It is hard and it is tough. Anger on behalf of somebody weaker than you strengthens your position as a leader. In the words of James Q. Wilson in *The Moral Sense*, "Anger is the necessary handmaiden of sympathy and fairness, and we are wrong to try to make everyone sweet and reasonable."[22]

In our politics today, the biggest threat we face is rejecting kindness not in favor of anger, but of contempt. As we have seen, contempt destroys unity and leads to permanent division. It's the political equivalent of using a weapon of mass destruction. In an arms race, it sometimes feels as though one must adopt this weapon. That is incorrect. In the long run, niceness and strength (with occasional righteous anger) are the right combination for effective, authoritative leadership and the best way to win—because in the long run, people are instinctively attracted to happy warriors who fight for others.

My orchestra went from one coercive leader to another. People hated them, but saw them as a necessary evil to meet the difficulties of managing a fractious workforce of artists. Likewise, we hear Americans on all sides say they don't like the status quo but believe we need to shake things up with no niceties—in other words, we need coercive leadership. This is false. Coercive leadership is a surrender to misery. A real solution to our problems, one that lasts and works for all of us, is *authoritative* leadership. I believe that's what we really want.

Maybe you're thinking I'm a Pollyanna, that there's no appetite in America for authoritative public leadership. Perhaps the last few years have beaten you down so much that you have become pessimistic or hopeless and have concluded that our new state of political nature is something like what Thomas Hobbes described as what life would be if left up to nothing but our own devices: "Nasty, brutish, and short."

I disagree. I think America is ready for unifying, authoritative, visionary leadership at all levels: in politics, media, and my own world of academia. We saw a desire for visionary leadership made manifest when Hawk Newsome took the microphone at a Trump rally on the National Mall and was embraced by many in the pro-Trump crowd. He tapped into a hunger for unity among those Trump supporters. Not everyone liked it. There were people in the audience who booed him. (Remember, we can't ever expect to bring along 100 percent.) But when they were presented with a compelling vision of a unified and opportunity-filled country from somebody with whom they disagreed, a big segment of those people said, "Wow, that's really great." The fifty-seven million people who viewed Hawk's speech online are further evidence of this desire for a better kind of leadership.[23]

That response should tell us something: authoritative

leadership touches hearts. It gives us what we crave more than revenge, even more than pure victory. It brings us a meaningful connection with our brothers and sisters.

How do we uncover and feed this hunger for more authoritative leadership in our nation today? For clues, we can look to our recent history. In the 1950s and 1960s, America was deeply divided over race relations. Conventional politicians believed that white America was not ready for or didn't care about civil rights for black Americans. Civil rights legislation in Congress stalled. Divisive, coercive leaders fed a political demand for segregation and resisted change.

Then along came one of the greatest authoritative leaders in American history, Dr. Martin Luther King Jr. He envisioned what escaped the eyes and even imaginations of many other leaders of his time: an America insistent on the common humanity and right to dignity of all people, no matter their race. He saw that deep down, below the surface, most white people, middle-class people, urban people—*most* people—wanted America to be a better country, one that lived up to the promise of the nation's founding. He saw that they would work to that end if only a leader would inspire them to do so.

King offered a vision of a unified future. Standing in the shadow of Abraham Lincoln on the National Mall, he declared "I have a dream that one day this nation will rise up and live out the true meaning of its creed: 'We hold these truths to be self-evident: that all men are created equal.' I have a dream that one day on the red hills of Georgia the sons of former slaves and the sons of former slaveowners will be able to sit down together at a table of brotherhood. . . . I have a dream that my four children will one day live in a nation where they will not be judged by the color of their skin but by the content of their character."

His was a deeply unifying message that touched the hearts not just of those gathered on the National Mall, but of millions of Americans who had not been part of the civil rights cause, yet deep in their hearts wanted to see King's vision realized, because it would make the United States a better country that lived up to its own stated values. Of course, the country did not change overnight. King was, in fact, broadly unpopular over much of his career.[24] But what made him such a profoundly impactful leader was that he saw—indeed, created—a hunger for civil rights that people didn't even know they had. By the end of his life, and especially after his death, that hunger became the norm for people of all races.

Going further back, we remember that authoritative public leadership was the secret to America's founding. In the 1770s, many colonists knew they were unhappy with King George III. They knew they hated the tea tax and the Stamp Act. But they didn't know they wanted to create a new country. I was amused to learn that my direct ancestor, John Brooks, was married in Boston on July 4, 1776. There is absolutely no evidence that he was agitating in any way for the birth of a republic.

The independence movement didn't begin until a group of visionary leaders like George Washington, Thomas Jefferson, and John Adams claimed that we could make a new kind of nation. They articulated a revolutionary vision of self-government, and by acting as authoritative leaders, they inspired their fellow men and women to take up together the cause of life, liberty, and—most radically—the pursuit of happiness. It is worth noting that many of these founders, such as Adams and Jefferson, agreed on little except the need for an exceptional new nation. Indeed, it was their disagreements as much as their agreements that created the American idea as we understand it today.

We find examples of such visionary catalysts in other parts of the world as well. For all its manifest problems, take the extraordinary case of modern Europe. For 1,500 years there had been fairly constant war on the European continent. Then, out of the rubble of World War II, the most destructive war in human history— waged by coercive leaders—a group of authoritative leaders envisioned a new way to bring about lasting peace and unity as a continent, because they saw and understood that there was an underlying hunger among Europeans for an end to conflict. They were right. For most of the seven decades since the end of World War II, Europe has been growing in prosperity, and inside the European Union, it has been free of war.

These examples demonstrate that the most lasting, most moral victories are propelled by authoritative leaders, not those who belittle, coerce, or polarize. When we land upon hard times, it is only natural to look for a coercive leader—one who will identify the enemy, shake up the status quo, and fight using any means necessary, dirty or clean. However, if we want to give ourselves the best chance to both recover from a crisis *and* build a future of lasting prosperity, we should look to authoritative leaders.

Our challenge, going forward, is to follow the visionary examples of Dr. King and our Founding Fathers, not the model of coercive leadership that has recently come to the fore in many nations. Doing so will take courageous leaders on the national stage, no doubt. It will take a willingness to rethink leadership. It will require leaders willing to take risks.

But the solution doesn't begin only with national figures in politics and culture. It also starts with us, who can be everyday authoritative leaders, whether at home, around the watercooler at work, or in our neighborhoods. We can exhibit the kind of leadership we wish to see from our country's public figures. As we practice authoritative leadership in our own lives, we will find ourselves better prepared to weather the storms we face as individuals, and as a nation.

Chapter 4
How Can I Love My Enemies If They Are Immoral?

For years, I complained that people no longer believed in moral truths.

Maybe this complaint is a natural "kids these days" lament of a grumpy middle-aged man, but I felt there was more to it than that. As *New York Times* columnist David Brooks (a friend but no relation) has written, "Morality was once revealed, inherited and shared, but now it's thought of as something that emerges in the privacy of your own heart." He cites the work of Notre Dame sociologist Christian Smith, who has interviewed hundreds of young people about their moral beliefs, finding that for most, morality is a foreign concept. Most are unwilling to make a moral pronouncement about acts as serious as drunk driving or adultery. In the words of one of Smith's interviewees, "I don't really deal with right and wrong that often."[1]

It's as if Nietzsche's *Beyond Good and Evil* were effectively supplanting the Bible, Koran, and Bhagavad Gita. I understand the temptation of young people to dismiss victimless crimes, but could anything be more dystopian than an entire generation that can't say things like drunk driving and infidelity are bad? Can America persist as a great nation with a population unwilling or unable to set a few standards of right and wrong? I don't think so, and wished things were different.

Be careful what you wish for. As the 2016 presidential campaign unfolded, everybody seemed to become a moralist. It started with the candidates themselves. Hillary Clinton famously condemned the moral turpitude of millions of Americans at a New York fund-raiser: "You know," she said, "to just be grossly generalistic, you could put half of Trump's supporters into what I call the basket of deplorables. Right? The racist, sexist, homophobic, xenophobic, Islamophobic—you name it. And unfortunately there are people like that." Meanwhile, throughout the campaign, Donald Trump was a geyser of moral condemnation on Twitter. In hundreds of posts, he explicitly labeled his opponents and critics "bad people," "evil," and "liars," among other things.

Of course, presidential candidates set the national tone, and political arguments—from television, to the dinner table, to even the campuses that were once bereft of moral absolutes—have turned into moral battlefields. Nothing is about honest disagreement; it is all about your interlocutor's lack of basic human decency. Thus, no one with whom you disagree is worth engaging at all. The result is contempt.

Now, playing the peacemaker, I find that *I* am the moral relativist. In arguments that would make a French existentialist philosopher blush on my behalf, I find myself saying, "Don't be so quick to say that *your* right and wrong is the only way to see things."

You can see I'm in a bit of a pickle here. I always believed that there are moral truths. I may not see them all clearly or be right in all my sentiments, but I think my views more or less reflect these truths—or at least, that is my aim. At the same time, I want Americans to be accepting of beliefs they don't hold, as part of a pluralistic but harmonious society. But if opposing points of view have an underlying basis in moral truth, doesn't someone have to be immoral, particularly on really contentious issues?

How can I engage with, let alone love, someone whom I believe to be immoral? Or are there no moral truths after all?

I met Jonathan Haidt in 2007. I was teaching public administration at Syracuse University; he was a social psychologist at the University of Virginia. I had just written a book about happiness, and organized a conference on the topic at the American Enterprise Institute, where I was a visiting scholar (and where later, I became president). Jon had written a book called *The Happiness Hypothesis* a couple of years earlier, which I read and loved. I invited him to my little conference, and we hit it off immediately. Later, Jon told me he was nervous about that conference. Why? Because AEI is known as a conservative outfit, and Jon considered himself a bona fide progressive. He didn't know how he would be treated, but he was pleasantly surprised that the event wasn't really ideological at all, and no one cared if he was a liberal or not.

The interaction came at a pivotal period for Jon in his career. While he was at AEI talking about happiness, his new research was looking at what is known as "moral foundations theory," which specifically addresses how conservatives and liberals differ in their moral views. Haidt was finding that certain ideas of morality are innate and that "the worst idea in all of psychology is the idea that the mind is a blank slate at birth."* His research showed that we are in fact born with particular moral foundations that make it easy for us to learn certain ideas of right and wrong, and hard to learn others.

---

* My mentor and intellectual hero, social scientist James Q. Wilson (who spent most of his career as a professor at Harvard and UCLA), argued that making moral judgments is the most natural thing for humans to do. In his 1993 book *The Moral Sense*, he held that morality is neither anthropologically based nor a cultural adaptation. Each of us comes into the world with a natural sense of the divine, a built-in sense of right and wrong. "The view that there is not a natural moral sense," he explained, began "when philosophers argued that the human mind was a *tabula rasa*" and that "everything, including morality, had to be learned." However, Wilson pointed out, modern science has shown us that "the child is an 'intuitive moralist.'" Newborns can express happiness, sadness, surprise, interest, disgust, anger, and fear, and within a few years of birth, children "will share toys, offer help, and console others who are in distress." They also have an innate sense of fairness. "Perhaps the first moral judgement uttered by the child is 'That's not fair!'" As adults, Wilson pointed out, "Much of the time our inclination toward fair play or our sympathy for the plight of others are immediate and instinctive, a reflex of our emotions more than an act of our intellect, and in those cases in which we do deliberate (for example, by struggling to decide what fair play entails or duty requires in a particular case), our deliberation begins, not with philosophical premises (much less with justification for them), but with feelings—in short, with a moral sense."

Using survey data for hundreds of thousands of individuals, Haidt was finding that there are in fact five
innate moral values that exist among humans of all
races and cultures, which he calls the "five foundations
of morality."[2] They are: (1) fairness, (2) care for others, (3) respect for authority, (4) loyalty to one's group,
and (5) purity or sanctity. (Later, he added liberty to
the list.) Haidt's research has shown that of these five
moral foundations, the first two—fairness and care—
are nearly universal. Except for sociopaths, almost
everyone—conservative or liberal, young or old, religious or nonreligious—believes in fairness and compassion to others.

Is it nature or nurture? People have disagreed on this
for millennia. One of my favorite arguments for the latter comes from Saint Augustine's classic *Confessions*,
written in AD 397. Suffice it to say, he was not of the
belief that babies are naturally good and moral: "No
one is free from sin . . . not even an infant whose span of
earthly life is but a single day."[3] Tough stuff. Augustine
confesses his own infant venality: "What then was my
sin at that age? Was it perhaps that I cried so greedily
for those breasts? Certainly if I behaved like that now,
greedy not for breasts, of course, but for food suitable
to my age, I should provoke derision and be very properly rebuked. My behavior then was equally deserving

of rebuke." In conclusion: "The only innocent feature in babies is the weakness of their frames; the minds of infants are far from innocent." Fortunately, Augustine was not a pediatrician. ("Your child is just naturally evil, ma'am.")

Modern scholars are a bit more forgiving than Augustine, finding evidence that the instinct to act fairly and with compassion toward others is with us from a young age. Let's start with fairness. In a 2011 study, researchers at Sweden's Uppsala University asked young children to distribute an odd number of rewards between two puppets, one of which had been helpful to a third puppet and one of which had been unhelpful.[4] The children routinely gave the helpful puppet the larger share of the rewards, explaining their distributions in terms of what would be fair given each puppet's behavior.

We're not just inclined to act fairly, however. We are also *actively disinclined* to violate principles of fairness. Psychologists from the University of Toronto have found that our bodies issue a negative physical response when we entertain the idea of cheating on a test, even if there is no risk of being caught. In an experiment involving undergraduate test takers, participants deciding whether or not to cheat—and who had been explicitly told that cheating would not be punished— had elevated heart rates, shortened breath, and sweaty palms.[5] In other words, we're even *physically* averse to behaving unfairly.

A commitment to the idea of fairness seems to be at least somewhat innate. Of course, that raises the question, What *is* fairness? At this point, the plot thickens.

We are all genetically programmed to believe in the moral values of fairness, but there are two different *expressions* of that shared moral value. The first expression can be called *redistributive fairness*, which holds that it is fair to redistribute rewards proportional to our needs. The game is rigged, and so you have to redistribute wealth because the rigging is inherently unfair. The second expression can be called *meritocratic fairness*, which holds that fairness means always matching reward to merit. You should get only what you earn, nothing for free, and you should not be able to take away something that somebody else earns. In the former expression, increasing equality is fair as a correction to an unfair playing field where children's start in life is determined by parents' wealth; in the latter, forcing equality is inherently *unfair* as a theft of the fruits of one person's labor to benefit another, robbing Peter to pay Paul.

We all believe in both types of fairness to some extent, but the proportions differ with respect to political ideology. Liberals tend to emphasize redistributive fairness, while conservatives put a greater emphasis on meritocratic fairness. That said, I've never met anyone on the left who thinks there's no such thing as merit. And even the most libertarian thinkers believe in *some* redistribution. The iconic conservative libertarian economist Friedrich Hayek wrote, in his seminal free-market text, *The Road to Serfdom*, "There is no reason why in a society which has reached the general level of wealth which ours has . . . security should not be guaranteed to all . . . there can be no doubt that some minimum of food, shelter, and clothing . . . can be assured to everybody. . . . Nor is there any reason why the state should not assist the individuals in providing for those common hazards of life against which, because of their uncertainty, few individuals can make adequate provision."[6]

In other words, if you're on the left, you most likely emphasize redistribution but also believe in merit. And if you're on the right, you probably emphasize merit but also believe in redistribution. These are different expressions of a shared moral value that is innate in who we are as people.

The same is true for the other value that all healthy humans share: compassion. Haidt's research shows that people all across the political spectrum are predisposed to place great importance on taking care of those in need and to dislike it when they see others harm the weak. "We all have a lot of neural and hormonal programming that makes us really bond with others, care for others, feel compassion for others, especially the weak and vulnerable," he says. "It gives us very strong feelings about those who cause [them] harm."

As with fairness, people on the left and right tend to emphasize different *expressions* of compassion. Liberals tend to show compassion for the weak by providing them with basic human needs like housing, food, and health care. Conservatives, by contrast, tend to see compassion as helping others to help themselves, through job training, wage subsidies, and work requirements for welfare. (Whether either liberals or conservatives live up to their beliefs in policy is another matter, of course.)

Despite this difference in emphasis, most conservatives also believe in direct assistance to the poor, while most liberals also believe in self-reliance. During his inaugural address as governor of California, Ronald Reagan declared, "We accept without reservation our obligation to help the aged, disabled, and those unfortunates who, through no fault of their own, must depend on their fellow man."[7] And during a 2012 speech to the National Urban League, Barack Obama declared that young people in disadvantaged communities need to stop hanging out and start doing homework, because "America says, 'we will give you opportunity, but you've got to earn your success.'"[8]

Public opinion polls show that most of us, left and right, agree with Presidents Reagan and Obama. A 2016 American National Election Studies survey found just 19 percent of working people (and 11 percent of nonworking people) support cutting "aid to the poor."[9] Meanwhile, a 2018 survey by the Foundation for Government Accountability asked Americans whether they "support requiring able-bodied adults to work, train, or volunteer at least part-time in order to receive welfare": 97 percent of Republicans and 82 percent of Democrats agreed.[10] Large majorities also supported work requirements for food stamps (Republicans, 95 percent; Democrats, 71 percent), Medicaid (Republicans, 90 percent; Democrats, 59 percent), and public housing (Republicans, 93 percent; Democrats, 68 percent). Democratic support for work requirements lagged behind Republican support, but it was still by far the majority view.

In sum, belief in compassion and fairness is encoded into the moral compass of almost all people. Those on the left and the right express those shared moral values differently, with emphasis on different aspects, but they agree with each other about the central moral values. The implication of these findings is both critically important and inescapably clear: nearly all of those who disagree with us are *not*, as we so often think, immoral; they simply express this morality in different ways.

So far, this is good news for people who want to find common ground between left and right. At this point, however, there is a major complication. The three other moral traits Haidt identified—respect for authority, loyalty to group or tribe, and purity or sanctity—are where conservatives and liberals diverge radically. Conservatives place a high importance on these values, while for most liberals, these are not priorities.

A few examples make this a bit clearer. In 1993, a controversy erupted when Army Lieutenant General Barry R. McCaffrey was visiting the White House during the first week of the Clinton administration. He was on his way out of the southwest gate of the White House complex, and a young White House aide was on her way in. The *Washington Post* reports, "McCaffrey said, 'Good morning.' The woman, he recalled in an interview, said, 'I don't talk to the military,' and stomped on by."[11]

I remember that liberals shrugged it off as no big deal—an unnecessary bit of petulance by the young woman, perhaps, but nothing to get upset about. But conservatives were outraged, and held the incident up as a sign of endemic lack of respect for the military by the left. McCaffrey (whom Clinton later appointed to a senior position on the Joint Chiefs of Staff) said that it did not reflect the feelings of the president, who had avoided the Vietnam draft. The story struck a nerve, because it was based on the reality that conservatives care more about respect for authority than liberals do.

The same is true with group loyalty. During his 2008 presidential campaign, a controversy erupted because Barack Obama did not wear an American flag pin on his lapel, like most candidates did in the period following the September 11, 2001, terrorist attacks. Obama had said earlier in an interview that he had stopped wearing the flag on his lapel after the Iraq war: "I decided I won't wear that pin on my chest," he said. "Instead, I'm going to try to tell the American people what I believe will make this country great, and hopefully that will be a testimony to my patriotism."[12] This sparked outrage on the right, and even some conspiracies based on fake quotes attributed to Obama about him not loving America. During one of the presidential debates, a voter asked Obama, "I want to know if you believe in the American flag. I am not questioning your patriotism, but all our servicemen, policemen, and EMS wear the flag. I want to know why you don't."[13]

For many liberals, Obama's decision seemed like no big deal, but for some conservatives it was seen as unpatriotic. The story took off because it played into a stereotype that, according to Haidt's research, is based in the reality that loyalty to one's group, including patriotism, is less important to people on the ideological left than it is to people on the ideological right. During the controversy, I remember a liberal colleague shaking her head in disbelief that anyone would care about something so trivial. And I remember conservative friends amazed that liberals didn't see the problem.

This is not to say that liberals don't love their country—of course they do. But they put less of an emphasis on overt patriotism than conservatives do. Take the recent controversy over NFL players kneeling during the national anthem. A 2017 poll found that 87 percent of conservatives agreed with the statement "NFL players should stand and be respectful during the national anthem," while only 33 percent of liberals agreed; 68 percent of conservatives also said the anthem protests made them less likely to watch football, while just 12 percent of liberals said so.[14]

I often conduct communications seminars for members of Congress. During one such session, when I was illustrating this point, I asked a Republican congressman from a very conservative southern district, "What's the first thing that pops into your head when I say 'flag burning'?" He replied without hesitation: "treason." A few weeks later, I was speaking with somebody I'm very close to who's on the political left, and I asked the same question. "What's the first thing that comes to mind when I say 'flag burning'?" His answer: "inadvisable."

Conservatives also put a different moral premium on the value of personal purity than liberals do, especially on sexual matters. Most evangelical Christians don't believe in sex before marriage. A recent poll found that 63 percent of unmarried evangelicals aged eighteen to twenty-nine who attend church weekly have never had sex, and 65 percent are committed to abstinence until marriage.[15] Most people on the left, by contrast, don't understand why anyone would consider premarital sex morally wrong. According to a 2003 Gallup poll, 80 percent of liberals say they believe premarital sex is morally acceptable, compared to 64 percent of moderates, and 42 percent of conservatives.[16] The difference is illustrated by a common bumper sticker Jon Haidt uses as an example of this point: YOUR BODY MAY BE A TEMPLE. MINE IS AN AMUSEMENT PARK. Ask yourself whether the person driving that car is a liberal or a conservative. The question pretty much answers itself, I think.

Conservatives look at all this and often conclude that liberals are less moral than they are, but the science shows this is not true. Liberals are not *less* moral; they simply have *fewer* moral foundations. According to Haidt's research, "Liberals have a kind of a two-channel, or two-foundation morality" while "conservatives have more of a . . . five-channel morality." All of us, regardless of where we sit on the political spectrum, care about social morality, treating others with fairness and compassion. By contrast, personal moral values, such as sexual purity, respect for authority, and tribal loyalty—to which conservative politicians often give greater emphasis—resonate deeply with only a part of the population.

When it comes to loyalty, authority, and purity, conservatives are from Mars, and liberals are from Venus. Or vice versa, I'm not sure. I just know it's different planets.

Our picture of morality is starting to come into focus. On compassion and fairness, most of the population is morally engaged. On authority, loyalty, and purity, you lose the liberals and have only the conservatives left.

There is one other area we need to discuss, which, morally, loses pretty much everybody. That's money. It's a funny thing in my world of think tanks and academics, especially among economists like me—and very especially among conservative economists: we talk as if money per se had moral salience. It doesn't.

By this I don't mean that people don't care about money; they obviously do. They will kill one another and risk their freedom for it. But a bank robber never says, "It was the principle that made me do it." He does it because he wants money. I have never looked at the numbers in my bank account and been moved emotionally, except back in my days as a musician when it was clear I wasn't going to make my rent.

Unfortunately, people in my world often forget this. Take, for example, the debate over the minimum wage. Many economists believe that raising the minimum wage is a bad instrument for achieving a worthy goal—namely, boosting the incomes of low-income Americans. This is because minimum-wage hikes make low-skill workers artificially more expensive to employ, which—many economists believe—destroys job opportunities for the people who need them most urgently.

In fighting minimum-wage increases, we often make an argument that goes something like this: "Raising the minimum wage is wrong because it increases the cost of labor. If you raise the cost of labor, businesses will respond by using less of it. Firms create jobs only when adding marginal workers will generate net revenue. So, if you raise the minimum wage, you are pricing cheap labor out of the market."

At this point, someone listening will often argue: "No one can live and support a family on $8 an hour. You don't think the billionaires who own Wal-Mart can afford to pay a few more dollars per hour? Of course they can." Who wins this debate? Not me. My interlocutor has made a fairness-and-compassion argument, invoking universal moral values. I made a money argument, which has no moral salience.

The right argument for me to make in fighting the minimum wage is one that defends the welfare and dignity of poor people who stand to lose their jobs. "We can't stand by while policies eliminate the jobs of the most vulnerable Americans." This is based in fairness and compassion. Then I must propose alternative policies to help the working poor, such as expanding wage subsidies, like the Earned Income Tax Credit, that do not kill jobs but rather create incentives for work.

The point is this: If you are making an argument about money, you are fighting a losing battle of moral math. You've eviscerated your own ability to make moral arguments when you start with money for the sake of money. Moral arguments beat economic arguments every time, because—whether we are liberal or conservative—we are all moral creatures who are encoded to value compassion and fairness.

When you are about to make an argument, ask yourself a question: Am I about to appeal to the majority, the minority, or no one (except perhaps a few conservative economists)?

There are three major lessons from the science of morality that I want to emphasize in order to take on the culture of contempt and bring people together.

1. Focus your arguments on the moral values we share—compassion and fairness—rather than those held by only one part of the population.

If you support stricter gun laws, rather than attacking those who disagree as caring more about guns than children, make the moral case that it's not fair that kids don't feel safe in their schools. If you oppose restrictions on Second Amendment rights, rather than attacking those who disagree for not caring about the Constitution, appeal instead to the same unifying moral values, by making the case that it is not fair to disarm vulnerable people and leave them unable to defend themselves from violence.

It's about more than just winning the debate. When we engage those who hold different opinions, we can unite people who may never agree on the specific issue by reminding them that we all agree we want to work for compassion and fairness. Focus on what unites us—our shared values—rather than just our own side's *expression* of shared values. When we start with the shared values themselves, we establish common moral ground, which then allows us to talk in a spirit of respect about our disagreement in the most effective way to express these values. Even without agreement, it strikes a blow against contempt.

Here is another way of thinking about this that I got from my friend, the bestselling author Simon Sinek. Every argument has a "why" and a "what." We have moral objectives (why) and we have policies to achieve those objectives (what). If you want to be a unifying and persuasive leader, you start by saying, "I share your *why* but I don't share your *what*. And I think that my *what* is more effective to meet your *why*. When it comes to morality, the thing I share with you is compassion and fairness. I don't reject your expression of compassion and fairness; I simply think I have a better way to meet our shared objectives of compassion and fairness." OK, maybe you don't say it in exactly those words because you're not a nerdy social scientist, but you get the idea.

Why does this distinction matter? People care about their "what" but aren't usually willing to sacrifice a relationship over it. But their "why" is written on their hearts. It is central to who they are as people—how they see themselves morally. Attack that and you are saying, "You are a bad person." For that you'll get a big, damaging fight.

Let's look at a few more practical examples. If you are a liberal trying to persuade conservatives to be more redistributionist, don't begin by attacking the idea of work requirements for welfare. Start by acknowledging your shared values—that we all believe that all people should be able to support themselves and a family with a hard day's work. Then you can make your case as to why that requires more direct assistance, like childcare, affordable housing, and paid family leave.

If you are a conservative and you want to convince liberals to be more supportive of work requirements for welfare, don't start by attacking redistribution. Start by acknowledging the value of the social safety net and your shared commitment to making sure that we take care of those who truly cannot take care of themselves. Then you can make the case that we want everybody to enjoy the purpose and meaning that comes from earning his or her success. If you take this approach, you're sending your liberal interlocutor a message: "I'm not waging war on your moral views. We share a common *why*, but we differ on the best *what* to reach our shared *why*." Your interlocutor will think, *OK, he's not attacking me or my core morality, so I can listen to this*, and then respond, "Of course I'm in favor of people working, because working is obviously better for a person than getting a check for doing nothing."

2. Be wary of manipulative leaders in politics and media who use the moral dimensions where we disagree as a wedge to divide us and fuel contempt.

We constantly hear conservative leaders using authority, loyalty, and purity arguments as evidence that liberals are immoral, unpatriotic reprobates because they don't emphasize these things. Liberal leaders scream back that conservatives are some sort of American Taliban because they *do* care about these things. Unifying leaders don't fool themselves into thinking that these moral dimensions don't matter or that the differences don't exist. Nevertheless, if progress is our goal, then emphasizing these dimensions is unproductive.

This is like trying to change someone else's taste buds. My wife and I mostly like the same foods, but not completely. I love cilantro, for example, and she doesn't. More than a tiny bit, it tastes like soap to her. This turns out not to be a mere preference; there is evidence that this is a genetic trait—kind of like our morals! Most nights when I'm at home, we eat dinner together and share our food as families generally do. We don't spend any time fussing about cilantro—whether it's delicious or tastes like soap—because there's no point. We simply don't put it in our shared food.

Make your moral discussions with most people like the cilantro at our family dinner. Say you have a really strong opinion that NFL players should stand for the national anthem. Your aunt disagrees; she thinks it's no big scandal for a player to kneel in protest, nothing to get worked up about. She argues that players' right to free expression is more important than a national symbol. You can go at her all the way through Thanksgiving dinner about how it *is* a big deal—that Americans have laid down their lives for the flag and that we should honor their sacrifice. What you are really arguing about, however, is authority and loyalty, moral dimensions on which you are just wired differently. You aren't going to change her mind through the force of argument any more than I will make my wife start liking cilantro by trying to force enough of it into her mouth.

In our conversations, we should be careful about going on the offensive over issues that rely on differing moral codes about obedience, patriotism, and pleasure. Furthermore, we should pay closer attention when politicians criticize people on the other side. Are they using our differing moral foundations to justify claims that the other side is worthy of contempt? If so, we owe it to our fellow Americans who disagree with us to recognize and reject this kind of rhetoric.

3. Divergent moral values are not a bug in the human system. They are a feature that can make us stronger.

Obviously, we can't avoid differing moral sensibilities entirely. Sometimes you get a little cilantro in your food, and sometimes you get a moral argument you disagree with, whether you like it or not. What is a unifying leader to do in that case? Celebrate and embrace ideological diversity! In fact, good leaders should purposively get out of their ideological bubbles and interact with those in other positions along the spectrum of personal morality in America.

This is not easy to do. Even in an age that celebrates diversity, most people assiduously avoid those who hold different moral values. Indeed, people avoid those with different values more than they do people of different racial backgrounds. In one study with undergraduate students, Haidt and his colleagues found that "in fraternity admissions, fraternity brothers were happy to admit people who were demographically different from themselves, although they avoided candidates who had strong moral or political values that differed either from the group as a whole, or from themselves as individuals." He also found that in choosing a study partner, most undergraduates did not care about racial differences, "but political/moral differences generally made a candidate less attractive."[17] Haidt's work is consistent with more recent research that shows the starkest dividing line in America today is not race, religion, or economic status, but rather party affiliation.[18] In fact, scholars at Stanford and Princeton have found that political partisans in America now take a more discriminatory view of those in the opposing party than they do of people of other races.[19]

This is not surprising. Humans have a natural tendency to go where we already feel comfortable and welcome. If you are an evangelical Christian, you are most comfortable with other evangelicals, who appreciate and share your values; if you are a secular humanist, you probably feel more comfortable hanging out with atheists and agnostics. If we want more unity and less contempt, however, we need to get out of our comfort zones, go where we are *not* welcome, and spend time talking and interacting with people with whom we disagree—not on lightweight stuff like sports and food, but on hard moral things.

Besides lessening contempt, there's another benefit to learning about other people's moral foundations: it makes life more fun. Feeling threatened or grossed out at the thought of other people's politics or their private lives just isn't all that enjoyable. Exposing yourself to other ways of thinking—even ideas or expressions of morality that directly contradict your own—makes it easier to cope with them emotionally.

Here's an example: I have very deep religious convictions as a Roman Catholic. My faith is truly at the center of my life, and I love it. However, I have spent a lot of time with people who are of other faiths and many with no faith at all. I have lots of atheist friends, and I've gotten to understand and respect their beliefs. This has made life happier and easier for me as I navigate the culture, and easier for me to lead an institution with hundreds of employees.

A couple of years ago, when driving into New York City from New Jersey a few weeks before Christmas, I saw a billboard by the side of the road. It featured the silhouettes of the three Wise Men approaching a stable, with the star brightly shining overhead. A calm, reassuring Christmas image, I thought, until I saw the words underneath: YOU KNOW IT'S A MYTH. THIS SEASON, CELEBRATE REASON! The billboard had been purchased by the American Atheists.

My reaction? I burst out laughing. Maybe it was supposed to shock me, even insult me. But I found it hilarious, not enraging. An atheist billboard is not going to shake my Catholic faith, and it certainly isn't going to turn me against my atheist friends. My years of exposure to their point of view is the reason I still laugh today when I think about it. Engagement to people with different moral values has given me the power not to be offended, even if others are seeking to offend.

We've learned that the people who disagree with us are not necessarily *immoral*. In most cases, they simply have different moral foundations. Knowing this can help us refrain from issuing absolute pronouncements on matters that amount to nothing more than honest and legitimate differences of opinion, thereby lessening our contempt for one another.

Challenging someone else's moral foundations is probably an exercise in futility. It certainly won't be successful in a political debate. However, I do want to make the argument that there is one person whose values you might conceivably alter: you. We have natural moral proclivities but also free will. Notwithstanding what we feel, we can choose what to believe. Where each of us sits by nature is not necessarily where we have to sit by choice. While someone else is not likely to change our morals, we can choose our own outlook and ideology, especially when we are presented with evidence that someone else's values make a lot of sense.

I believe this because I am living proof of it. In many ways, I am genetically liberal. I don't feel an instinctive respect for authority, loyalty, or purity. After much reflection, however, I have decided that personal purity in the conservative sense is better for me and my loved ones. Similarly, loyalty to country and respect for authority are better, even though they don't come naturally to me. I am by nature redistributionist, but after years of studying economics, I have come to believe that free enterprise is the most effective way to help the poor. (Although I still strongly support government safety nets.)

My wife, Ester, is another example. She is European, with European sentiments and European reactions to all kinds of things. Still, she thinks the American way of life is, for the most part, better. She thinks that the American tendency to attribute success to hard work and personal responsibility is superior to the European tendency to assume that the game is rigged. Against her nature, she consciously has embraced an American moral outlook.

It's hard, but you can do that, too. You may be genetically predisposed to a conservative, five-channel moral foundation, but that doesn't mean you have to be a conservative if your intellect tells you otherwise. Think deeply. Listen to the other side. Reflect on what others are saying. Then ask yourself not just how you *feel*, but what you *think* is right. We're not slaves. We're not shackled to a pipe in the basement of our own built-in genetic morality. In his book *The Birth of the Mind*, the eminent brain scientist Gary Marcus writes, "'Built-in' does not mean unmalleable; it means organized in advance of experience." When it comes to our moral outlook, Marcus says, "Nature provides a first draft, which experience then revises."[20]

It is up to each of us to create the next drafts of our moral minds. We should constantly be evaluating whether our particular expression of our moral values is the right one, much less the *only* legitimate expression of those values. Doing so requires the humility to recognize that none of us has a monopoly on truth. The left favors redistribution; the right, meritocracy. But if we had a completely redistributionist society we'd be the Soviet Union; if we had a complete meritocracy, millions would be starving. There is a sweet spot between the two and we should all be searching together to find it.

Too many of us are like the Pharisee in Luke's Gospel who prays, "God, I thank You that I am not like other people—robbers, evildoers, adulterers—or even like this tax collector."[21] We should be more like the tax collector who, Luke tells us, "would not even look up to heaven, but beat his breast and said, 'God, have mercy on me, a sinner.'"

Chapter 5
The Power and Peril
of Identity

I am going to give you a list of one-sentence demographic identities of four people. As you read them,
knowing nothing else, form a mental picture, and ask
yourself what you feel about each person.

1. A Spanish-speaking immigrant woman, raised in
   poverty in a dictatorship, who comes to America
   as a young adult and works a minimum-wage job.

2. A politically conservative young man from an
   upper middle-class family, who studies at an Ivy
   League university.

3. A farmhand in rural Idaho, who spends his days
   driving a combine and his free time hunting and
   fishing.

4. A girl, orphaned at birth in a small village in China, who later winds up against all odds living in the United States.

These identities probably evoke a swift reaction in you, especially during this incredibly polarized time in American politics. Without knowing anything about these people except these brief descriptions, you are probably positively disposed toward one or two but indifferent or even hostile toward the others. If I asked you what these four people have in common, your answer would probably be, "Next to nothing." This is normal. Demographic and experiential "branding"—identification, by oneself or others, with a certain group or stereotype—has become extremely common.

There used to be a joke that if someone belongs to one of the following three groups, you will know it within ten seconds of meeting him or her: Harvard grad, former Marine, or vegan. These identities are so strong that it's nearly impossible not to announce them somehow. That's increasingly true for everyone else as well. People brand themselves in terms of demographic characteristics and selected life experiences to bond quickly with others in an anonymous society that can be cold and lonely. Identity can give a new student at a university far from home, or a twentysomething new in the workforce—or any of us—a shortcut to a sense of community and belonging. It is also how we figure out who's a friend and who's not. We use demographic identities to decide whether people are worth meeting and getting to know.

Our tools for establishing and ascertaining identity have become extremely efficient and have changed fundamental aspects of our social lives. Back when I was single, you got to know someone initially by going out for coffee or a meal. Do we have values in common? Do we see the world in the same way? Finding the answers took a couple of hours and a few bucks. Today, we have eliminated many of these transaction costs. On social media, we can sort possible mates by one-sentence identities and weed out all the people who are a bad match on this basis. Similarly, we can curate our friendships based on a picture and a few words of identity.

This is progress, right?

Richard LaPiere wanted to understand racism against the Chinese.

In the early twentieth century, discrimination against people of Chinese origin was a major social problem in the United States. From their arrival as migrant laborers during the Gold Rush of the nineteenth century, the Chinese had experienced bigotry and exclusion. People derisively referred to them as "coolies" and mocked their strange features, clothes, food, and language. Newspapers published by William Randolph Hearst popularized the term "Yellow Peril" to describe the danger of an invading horde of Chinese immigrants, and Hollywood capitalized on this fear with a series of movies featuring the murderous Chinese supervillain, Dr. Fu Manchu. Towns throughout the country passed discriminatory measures against the Chinese, and the U.S. Congress enacted laws that restricted Chinese immigration. The arrival of the Great Depression exacerbated these racial tensions. By the 1930s, discrimination against Chinese people was deep-seated, legal, and widespread.

Richard LaPiere was a sociology professor at Stanford University. He was determined to find the roots of this discrimination—as well as what would break it down and bring people of different races together in harmony.

LaPiere noticed that many people expressed discriminatory attitudes in surveys, but these were theoretical. In the 1930s, most Americans lived in homogeneous communities, with little exposure to different races. He wanted to know if their behavior when they met Chinese people matched their attitudes on a survey. Racism, he noted, could be either more or less pronounced in person than in theory.

LaPiere was an optimist about humanity. He thought we might confess racist attitudes but not act that way in real life. For example, he wrote, if hundreds of people were hypothetically asked whether they would give up their seat on a streetcar to a woman from an ostracized ethnic group, many might say no. The problem, LaPiere noted, is that the theoretical woman is different from a "woman of flesh and blood" and the respondent's "verbal reaction . . . does not involve rising from the seat or stolidly avoiding the hurt eyes of the hypothetical woman and the derogatory stares of other street car occupants." Presented with a real, live person, he hypothesized, most would probably behave differently than they told researchers they would.

This is the opposite of what people often assume today. The common assumption is that people mouth nonracist ideals and claim to embrace diversity but betray their bigotry, often in subtle ways, when faced with actual people different from themselves.

Which side is closer to being right about most Americans? LaPiere figured out an ingenious way to determine the answer. He recruited a young Chinese university student and his Chinese wife to help him. "Both were personable, charming and quick to win the admiration and respect of those they had the opportunity to become intimate with," he wrote. While both spoke fluent

English, "they were foreign born Chinese, a fact that could not be disguised." They stopped at what he described as "the 'best' hotel in a small town well-known for its narrow and bigoted 'attitude' towards Orientals," and went in to ask for a room. When the Chinese couple approached the front desk, he wrote, the clerk "accommodated us without a show of hesitation."

Afterward, LaPiere phoned the same hotel and asked if they would be willing to accommodate an important Chinese gentleman. "The reply was an unequivocal 'No.'"

Provocative, to be sure, but not proof in any scholarly sense, because it was only one case. So Professor LaPiere decided to undertake a systematic study.[1] Over a period of two years, between 1930 and 1932, he and the Chinese couple traveled over ten thousand miles back and forth across the United States and up and down the Pacific coast. On their journey they visited 251 establishments (67 hotels and 184 restaurants) and tracked how they were treated.

The results? "We met definite rejection from those asked to serve us just once," he wrote. They were turned away at a "rather inferior auto-camp." But that same night, he said, they found accommodations in "a more pretentious establishment . . . with an extra flourish of hospitality." Indeed, he wrote, at 72 of the 184 restaurants they visited—some 40 percent of them—the Chinese couple were not only accommodated but actually received what he judged to be above-average service. As a result, he wrote, "although they began their travels in this country with considerable trepidation, my Chinese friends soon lost all fear that they might receive a rebuff."

Having found little discrimination in practice, on their return, LaPiere mailed a conventional attitudinal survey to all the establishments they had visited, asking "Will you accept members of the Chinese race as guests in your establishment?" The available answers were Yes, No, and Depends upon the circumstances.

Of the 128 responses he received, 92 percent of the restaurants and 91 percent of the hotels said that, no, they would *not* serve guests of the Chinese race. All but one of the others said it would depend on the circumstances. The single "yes" came from the woman proprietor of an autocamp, whose returned survey, LaPiere wrote, was "accompanied by a chatty letter describing the nice visit she had had with a Chinese gentleman and his sweet wife during the previous summer"!

Let's consider what LaPiere had learned. For the vast majority who said they would discriminate, the couple was known by nothing more than their demographic identity. For the proprietor of the campground who

wrote the letter, the Chinese visitors were not a hypothetical abstraction. She had fond memories of the lovely
Chinese couple who had spent time at her camp. To her,
they were real people with real human stories, not just a
demographic identity.

Even those who said they would never, under any
circumstance, serve Chinese people *did so when faced
with real Chinese people*. Their practical human interactions with the Chinese couple overcame their theoretical prejudice.

These days, we frequently hear that most people today
have unconscious bias, that they think they don't discriminate, but in real life they actually do. The LaPiere
study supports the opposite idea. People are more hostile
to others in the abstract than when they meet them in
person. As a rule, theoretical discriminators, when they
come face-to-face with an actual person, actually *don't*
discriminate. It's much easier to dehumanize the "other"
when you don't see a human face, when someone is reduced to a demographic identity. When you meet actual
people and learn a little of their human story, you feel
connection—and connection destroys discrimination.

The lesson is that when people are reduced to a set
of fixed group characteristics, rather than appreciated as
individuals with shared humanity, unity is undermined
and contempt is made that much easier to express.

When LaPiere asked proprietors whether they would serve hypothetical "members of the Chinese race," he reduced the couple to their racial identity. He took away their full humanity. But showing up at the proprietor's establishment with a flesh-and-blood Chinese couple restored their humanity and their human story. People responded with warmth, because being confronted with the humanity of others curtails our capacity for hostility.

Why is that? An encounter with an individual person with a name and a face evokes our natural empathy and compassion. (The next chapter will explain the biology behind this fact.) For most people, empathy and compassion overwhelm prejudice and discrimination. It's not that prejudice or discrimination don't exist; they do, and can't be imagined away. But the key to overcoming prejudice and discrimination is not to double down on what makes people different; rather, it is to undermine prejudice with something more powerful: the empathy and compassion we all naturally feel when interacting with actual people and connecting with them as fellow humans.

As a social scientist, I found the LaPiere result fascinating, but it captured my imagination in much more than a theoretical way.

Think back to the question I posed at the outset of

this chapter, about your impressions of the four people based on their divergent demographic profiles: the Spanish-speaking immigrant woman, the conservative kid at an Ivy League school, the farmer in Idaho, and the orphaned Chinese girl.

It turns out that was a trick question. Those four people are my wife of twenty-seven years and our three children. Admittedly, we are way out on the tail in intra-family diversity. (Once when one of my kids was little, he described another family in the neighborhood as "one of those families where they look alike and all speak the same language.") What do we have in common? Intense love for one another, *which is the one thing that ultimately matters.*

Here's my point: identity obscures as much as it illuminates. It can create a quick sense of belonging among strangers, but it can just as easily create dividing lines where they should never exist, severing the human connections we can and should have with others and fomenting our culture of contempt.

This observation has helped me in my day-to-day work. As a social scientist, I routinely come across piles of data on the views of college professors, administrators, and students toward politically right-leaning people. It's not pretty. We're seen as immoral and heartless, and in theory, we are not welcome in many academic institutions. As I mentioned before, it can be stressful to speak on campuses. It isn't fun to feel unwelcome.

But when I show up and meet with students and faculty face-to-face and share my story as a person instead of just my political identity, I am virtually never treated unkindly. On the contrary, people are nearly always kind and welcoming, even when they disagree with me. Recently, I gave a talk at one of the most famously progressive campuses in America about connecting with others. Afterward, as a student was leaving, she said, "I came ready to fight, but I really connected with that speech." That made me truly happy, because a human connection was my objective.

As a social scientist, I try to live according to what I see in the research, and one of the reasons I have committed myself to speaking on campuses is Richard LaPiere's study. Coming face-to-face with people who hold discriminatory attitudes often breaks down their bigotry. This is consistent with a growing body of research that confirms much of what LaPiere discovered all those decades ago.

Here's how I could ruin these campus visits: I could come out with my political identity lit up like a Christmas tree. "Hey, guys, I'm a proud conservative! Get over it! *Ha ha, liberal tears!*" That would swamp my human connection with the audience, which is precisely

the problem with identity politics today, which emphasizes people's membership in a particular group, be it
political, religious, ethnic, or something else. It inevitably leads to less, not more, love.

It's important to recognize that this is true both
when we talk about ourselves and when we talk about
others. By defining ourselves in terms of unbridgeable
differences (I am conservative; you are not), we put our
common human stories out of reach for those who disagree with us. Likewise, by defining those with whom
we disagree as nothing more than a set of disembodied
characteristics (you are a liberal, nothing more), we put
their humanity out of our own reach. Much of the tribalism in our society today is due to the increasingly rigid
identities we both assume and assign to others.

Trying to understand others by going beyond demographic identity may seem sensible and straightforward to you, but I should note that not everyone buys
my line of reasoning. A common criticism of this kind
of argument is that, in fact, people cannot identify with
historically oppressed people and have no right even to
try. For example, because I am white and not an immigrant, the argument goes, I can neither understand
the experiences of nor say I can relate to historically
marginalized people—including the Chinese couple in
LaPiere's study. Under this kind of thinking, it is imma-

terial that I have met many immigrants and know lots of people of Chinese origin (in fact, my wife is the former and my daughter is the latter). Because of my personal demographic identity and lack of "lived experience," some would say, I should shut up.

It's true that my socioeconomic, cultural, political, racial, and religious background is not the same as others', and there *are* ways in which my understanding of those who are different from me is limited. However, none of that is an argument for keeping quiet and walling ourselves off. On the contrary, it's an argument for more radical diversity, in which we obliterate the "what" distinctions and strive to understand the shared moral "why" of our lives as brothers and sisters.

Reliance on demographic identity hurts unity. But wait, you might be thinking, don't demographic identities create extremely strong, tight-knit communities? Little Italy in New York, Chinatown in San Francisco, or Little Ethiopia in Washington, DC, all immediately come to mind as places with broadly homogeneous yet strong and vibrant communities. People gravitate to communities with shared demographics; as Nobel Prize–winning economist Thomas Schelling noted in his research, this is often how people naturally sort themselves.[2]

Self-sorting can make life easier for people in marginalized communities, but membership in a demographic group is not what we need to bring the *country* together, let alone the world. To understand this, we need to turn to the work of Harvard political scientist Robert Putnam, author of the brilliant book *Bowling Alone: The Collapse and Revival of American Community.* Putnam introduced millions to the concept of social capital, the "connections among individuals—social networks and the norms of reciprocity and trustworthiness that arise from them."[3]

There are two kinds of social capital. The first is *bonding social capital,* which is "inward looking" and tends to "reinforce exclusive identities and homogeneous groups."[4] Examples of bonding social capital come from things like having gone to the same university, ethnic similarity, or belonging to a specific religious denomination. Belonging to these sorts of groups builds cohesion—but only among those who share a narrow identity. This kind of bonding can provide social and psychological support for individuals, but it ultimately serves to entrench division based on demographic difference. It defines "us," but also, just as important, "them."

By contrast, *bridging social capital* is that which is born out of embracing those who don't fall into one's specific camp. Rather than relying on demographic characteristics, bridging social capital "can generate broader identities and reciprocity."[5] Bridging social capital is built on our common humanity; it emphasizes how we are alike rather than how we are different.

Like social capital, identity can be either bonding or bridging. *Bonding identity* describes how you and I are alike in some specific demographic way but differ from the broader society. For me, Roman Catholicism is a bonding identity. I have a bunch of friends with whom I have this in common. If you came to a dinner party with my Catholic friends and you are a Buddhist, it would be tricky to follow a lot of the conversation, and it might not feel very inclusive. Identity politics, which makes claims based on distinction from the whole, is based on bonding identity.

Bridging identity looks for my common humanity and experience with you, notwithstanding our demographic differences. It generally militates against identity politics as currently defined. While bonding identity tells some "what" about you that someone else can share, bridging identity is the "why" that unites you with all other people.

My own understanding of this comes from a friend, john a. powell, professor of law and African American studies and ethnic studies at the University of California–

Berkeley.* john's thinking has had a big influence on my own.

I should note that john's bonding identities could not be more different from my own. He grew up in Detroit; I'm from Seattle. He is black; I am white. He was the first person in his family to attend college; until I was thirty, I was the first person in my family *not* to go to college. john is an avowed progressive; I am not. But these characteristics are just the "what" of john and me. The important story is in the "why" that we share with each other. He is a warrior for the equality of human dignity and has dedicated his work to this cause; this is my "why" as well. We met in the course of this work some years ago, on a national commission to find pathways out of poverty. Because of our shared "why," we got on like a house on fire.

"I think people are not only not building bridges anymore, I think they're blowing them up and then taking hard stances," john tells me. "Breaking" occurs "when people claim themselves in opposition to another group, and the other group's a categorical evil." Much like contempt, breaking is not a passive act. As john defines it, breaking is "affirmatively attacking 'the other.' And . . . as we break in a serious way, we actually define

---

* john a. powell writes his name using all lowercase letters.

ourselves by our breaking. And so I define myself by the groups I hate." To my ear, this is an amazingly trenchant description of the dark side of identity politics.

What is happening more and more frequently, john believes, is that "we find out we have different perspectives, different cultures, and the perception is, the other person's wrong. . . . We tend to demonize people who think differently than us, without even spending time to say, 'How did you get there? What did you have for breakfast? Do you have children?'" We speed past the questions that would help us get to know another person's story and instead immediately look to the places of greatest difference and disagreement. As a result, we cripple our ability to locate areas of common ground that do exist.

The phenomenon of breaking is consistent with scholarship on the concept of "othering." As University of New South Wales professor Anthony Zwi maintains, othering is a process in which a person secures his or her own bonding identity by distancing or stigmatizing the identity of someone else.[6] Much like breaking, othering creates a hard line between "us" and "them" by making any kind of difference—whether skin color, socioeconomic status, political views, or anything else—a dividing line. The danger of othering, says john, is that we end up making caricatures of others because we never come into contact with them—and once we go down that road, he cautions, "we're not a long way from doing all kinds of terrible things to each other."

There is an alternative to breaking, though, and for this, john uses the same term as Putnam: "bridging." Rather than pushing away the "other" because of difference, bridging initiates contact. While it does not demand that we set aside every point of difference, bridging at its core *does* demand that we see and acknowledge the other person's humanity. It does not ignore difference, but it gives pride of place to what we hold in common. What does bridging look like in practice? john recalls for me an example from his own life.

He had gotten to know a woman named Sally, who lived on the streets of Berkeley, and he would occasionally give her money. But one day, when he asked if she needed anything, her request wasn't for food or cash. "I wondered if you could give me a hug," he remembers her saying sheepishly. john hesitated, but as he later explained, he realized Sally was really saying she needed to share john's humanity instead of being treated as a charity case. A hug unifies and says, "We are both people with dignity, capable of love." Sally was asking john to take her beyond the identity of a homeless beggar. He hugged her. There were any number of reasons why he could have chosen to break instead of bridge with Sally.

She was poor, disheveled, uneducated, and of low social status; he was none of those things. But by focusing on their common humanity rather than their marked differences in identity, the pair arrived at a place of profound unity.

What happened after this exchange, though, is just as instructive. Colleagues made fun of john because of his "homeless girlfriend." This reveals a sobering truth. "Sometimes," says john, "there's a cost associated with bridging. And sometimes, the cost can be quite high." In some cases, it's minor, like being ribbed by your friends. Other times, it's steeper, such as the social exclusion imposed on political progressives and conservatives these days by their own camps for refusing to vilify the other side. In the most serious cases, some pay the ultimate price for bridging. john reminds me that, during the Rwandan genocide, some Hutus who refused to kill their Tutsi neighbors were themselves killed by members of their own group for a lack of loyalty. Bridging, like warm-heartedness, takes courage.

When we break, emphasizing the bonding identities that divide us, we quickly lose sight of the humanity of others. This enables the kind of contempt and division that have become so pervasive in America. On the other hand, as john observes, "When we're faced with real people, with real contact, then the complexity comes in."

It's much harder to "other" others when we see them as fully human. The important lesson here is not that our differences are trivial or better off never discussed. It is that if we want to overcome a culture of contempt, we must look to what we have in common *before* we look to what makes us distinct. We have to bridge, not break.

To be sure, bridging is hard work and is by no means guaranteed by the existence of demographic diversity. Putnam himself notes that simply throwing people with strong bonding identities together can be counterproductive. His own research shows that circumstances that lend themselves to bridging—increases in immigration or ethnic diversity—sometimes actually reduce social solidarity and trust in the short run.[7] Putnam examined studies on countries around the world as well as survey data from thousands of Americans in forty different counties, cities, and towns. He found that in communities where ethnic and socioeconomic diversity is greater, "trust (even of one's own race) is lower, altruism and community cooperation rarer, friends fewer."[8] Countries with high levels of heterogeneity were found to have lower levels of social trust. Diverse groups in work contexts sometimes experienced lower cohesion and satisfaction. It would seem that, at least in the short run, bridging may hurt the cause of harmony more than it helps.

This does *not* mean we should abandon the cause of unity among different groups, however. It just means achieving harmony doesn't happen by itself; it takes skill and work. All of us who seek to heal our communities need to provide more "social glue" among groups. We can't leave it up to chance for communities to mix and create bridging identities. That requires leadership that brings different people together around shared moral purpose and a recognition that we all seek love and dignity. Bridging can be successful, but only when we purposively discard divisive identities in favor of our common stories and shared humanity, and help others to do likewise.

To see this, consider the case of marriage equality. This is still a hot-button issue, so try to suspend your opinions for or against gay marriage for a moment, and simply consider how the marriage-equality movement succeeded in dramatically changing public opinion in just the past few years. Broad exposure to gay people as people with ordinary lives helped turn national opinion in favor of same-sex marriage. For many years, there was wide awareness of gay identity without much popular support. But as it gradually became possible to be "out" without being ostracized or attacked, millions of gay people were able to make the argument to acquaintances that they only wanted that which their fellow citizens also wanted—civil rights, love, commitment, security, and family—and, conversation by conversation, they were able to overcome antipathy to same-sex marriage. By telling a bridging story rather than focusing on how their sexual identity made them different from most other Americans, the gay community transformed public opinion.

The critical lesson from this example and from Putnam is that *how* we bridge matters just as much, if not more, for unity than the bridging itself. Forcing people together but emphasizing our differences can be toxic. However, if we bring people together and emphasize our common stories, we can discover the new and broader "we" required to overcome mutual contempt.

In sum, what we typically think of as identity, as encapsulated in modern identity politics, is just one kind of identity: bonding identity. It identifies a common characteristic that distinguishes one group from others. In its most negative form, bonding identity can lead to "us versus them" breaking behavior, "othering" by those inside or outside the group—obviously a key part of the current culture of contempt. In LaPiere's research, race was this kind of identity. It could be used to bond a certain subgroup but was also used to "other" Chinese people.

Rather than rejecting identity per se, however, we

should expand our understanding of it to embrace bridging identity, which looks for common humanity across divergent characteristics. Bridging identity is what makes us, in the clichéd phrase, "embrace diversity"—and do so with love and pleasure. It's what our hearts truly desire in a divided world.

Great and virtuous leaders from all walks of life can take a strong bonding identity—one based on a shared "what"—and turn it into a bridging identity—a common moral "why." Let me give an example.

California's Los Angeles County is home to 1,100 street gangs with more than eighty-five thousand members. These are criminal enterprises that commit violent crimes and victimize entire communities. Why do young people join? Because the gangs provide belonging and bonding identity to people who are growing up amid drug addiction, unemployment, and homelessness. This is exactly how bonding works—forging strong connections among one particular group for the sake of belonging and protection against outsiders.

Such a bond comes at a steep price, however. Membership in a gang becomes the cornerstone of a young person's identity, demarcating social groups and dictating where one is welcome, down to the neighborhoods in which one can safely walk. To cross these metaphoric and physical boundaries can be fatal. Gang members are frequently victims of violence and have high rates of incarceration. It is an incredibly dangerous lifestyle.

This is a reality with which Father Greg Boyle, a Catholic priest living in the Los Angeles neighborhood of Boyle Heights, is all too familiar. He has celebrated funeral Masses for more than two hundred young people killed by gang violence. Fortunately, Father Boyle does more than officiating at funerals. He also works to make them less common, by breaking down the bonding identities that keep the city's gangs at war with one another, by showing the young people he meets a bridging identity that demonstrates that they are more similar than they are different. He does so by offering gang members opportunities for honest, legal work.

It all started at Homeboy Bakery, an enterprise founded by Boyle in 1992 to offer a way out to young people trapped in gang life.[9] Once a single store, the organization, known as Homeboy Industries, now maintains a citywide presence. As Boyle puts it, many of the youths who want to get off the streets "know to come to Homeboy when they are ready to 'hang up their gloves.'" They begin in the bakery (or one of the organization's other businesses, such as a café or screen-printing shop) to gain needed experience before moving on to a different job. But there's a catch: When gang members start out at Homeboy, they are expected to work alongside their rivals—nearly unthinkable in any other context. By engaging in shared tasks, Homeboy's young employees are able to see past their gang identities and realize that, just maybe, they aren't so different from one another.

In Boyle's words, young people are given "a chance to work with their enemies," and the effect of deemphasizing gang identities in favor of shared work and shared human stories is profound. By bringing together people who might have killed one another previously, by forcing them to confront the fact that they have a great deal in common, a crucial dissonance is created. According to Boyle, people still in the gangs ask their former gang members, "How can you work with that guy?" Though answering that question "will be awkward, clumsy, and always require courage," he says, the fact that the question is asked "jostles the status quo." Just how much has Father Boyle jostled the status quo? Enough that Homeboy Industries now reaches more than ten thousand former gang members in Los Angeles every year with a variety of services, from tattoo removal to anger management and parenting classes. Isolating difference is much harder to maintain when those we view with contempt stand before us as real people, imbued with whole, human stories.

Boyle is quick to tell me that the organization is not able to offer help to all who need it, only those who seek it out. In this, there is an important lesson—that emphasizing shared humanity over demographic differences is an *active choice*. If we wish to push back against what makes us different, we can't wait for someone else to do the bridging. But if we are willing to get closer to those we view with contempt or those who view us with contempt, like the young people under Father Boyle's care do, love and reconciliation will follow.

There are several key lessons to remember from this chapter if you want to fight the culture of contempt and seek to unify our communities, nation, and world.

My argument is not that demographic characteristics should be dismissed. They exist, and there is nothing wrong with that. Rather, we need to exercise caution in using them as a source of bonding identity, because this isolates us from others in the out-group as much as it unites us to those in our in-group. Likewise, it is dangerous to define others solely with respect to a bonding identity. While it may be descriptively true, it tends to dehumanize, to reduce another person to one dimension.

It is especially important for leaders who want to unite others to use their demographic identities sparingly. It is so tempting to get in front of a group with your own characteristics and say, "I'm one of you, not one of them!" It's the easiest way to get applause, but it sets us on the wrong path if harmony amid diversity is our goal.

There is a hierarchy of virtue for leaders today in a country driven apart by contempt. The worst are the "breakers," who seek to gain strength by driving people apart. They use the language of othering and exploit identity politics to define outsiders. This is the dominant strain today in national politics on both the left and right. You probably don't like that status quo, or you wouldn't be reading this book. Join me in committing to avoiding this practice. Don't support it on your political side.

In the middle are "bonders," who don't necessarily seek to profit from division, but do little to foster true unity because they use identity to strengthen links to their own groups. While not ill intentioned, they still neglect the opportunity to bring people together across divisions, which marginalizes others. In my opinion, this is a waste of leadership.

The ideal leaders today—whom we need more urgently than at any time in my life—are "bridgers," men and women dedicated to a radical embrace of diversity. These are leaders of all political stripes who see common human stories all around them and are determined to bring people together. Connection is found when we view one another as individuals with stories and dignity, just like ourselves. Bridging allows us to engage constructively with others when philosophical and ideological differences exist. While strong ties with those who share bonding identities with us are not all bad, it is only when we extend an open hand to those with different characteristics that the kind of trust necessary for solidarity can develop.

For both the left and right, then, unity requires us to see one another *as people* first and foremost. It requires us to identify our shared "why" and our common human stories before looking to any divided "what." This is not to say that we should dismiss our differences and the ways in which those differences have resulted in harder lives for some and easier lives for others. Rather, it is to say that when we learn to see others—especially those with whom we disagree—as being just as deserving of dignity and the chance to pursue happiness as we are, only then can we build bridges in the face of differences.

That's the secret for overcoming division and the culture of contempt that is permeating our country today. It's easy to have contempt for the "other," liberals or conservatives, Trump supporters or Black Lives Matter activists. It's much harder to have contempt for real people with names and faces and human stories. When we encounter one another as individuals and tell our stories, we overwhelm contempt with something more powerful: love.

So let's tell some stories.

Chapter 6
Tell Me a Story

One of the most famous *Saturday Night Live* sketches of all time is "More Cowbell," from the year 2000. Christopher Walken plays famed record producer Bruce Dickinson, in the recording studio with the band Blue Öyster Cult. As the group tries to lay down tracks for a new song, band member Gene Frenkle (played by Will Ferrell) ruins the first take by loudly banging on a cowbell. Dickinson steps into the studio and tells the band that what will really improve the track is . . . more cowbell. The same thing happens on the second try—and the third. Each time, Dickinson demands more cowbell, exactly the opposite of what is needed. Dickinson explains his reasoning: "Guess what. I got a fever! And the only prescription is *more cowbell*!"

Art mirrors life. At least, life as an economist frequently looks like that *SNL* sketch. We economists are trained to use data and evidence to make fact-based arguments about policy that convince others. This is based on the assumption of the "rational individual," who changes his mind in response to hard evidence, following John Adams's maxim: "Facts are stubborn things; and whatever may be our wishes, our inclinations, or the dictates of our passions, they cannot alter the state of facts and evidence."[1]

So what do we do when we put forth the best evidence and people still aren't convinced? We copy Bruce Dickinson: more cowbell—er, more data! If they weren't convinced by the evidence at first, then the only prescription is more evidence.

It never works. On the contrary, it often makes things worse. During the early years of my academic career, I never really seemed to convince anyone who didn't already agree with me that my arguments were worth considering. To use the example from earlier chapters, I would go on and on about the evidence of low-wage jobs lost because of minimum-wage increases, and the only heads nodding in agreement would be people who already thought minimum-wage increases were a flawed idea. So I'd reinforce the argument with more data, more facts, more evidence. The unpersuaded just looked at me as if I were stone-hearted or corrupted by some big corporation.

It took a few years for me to figure out that my whole working premise was incorrect. Fact-based arguments don't persuade people very well at all, it turns out, because people don't work like computers, updating their beliefs in response to the highest-fidelity data. All the way back in 1898, the social scientist Thorstein Veblen explained the faulty assumptions of conventional economic arguments in an article titled "Why Is Economics Not an Evolutionary Science?":

> The hedonistic conception of man is that of a lightning calculator of pleasures and pains, who oscillates like a homogeneous globule of desire of happiness under the impulse of stimuli that shift him about the area, but leave him intact. He has neither antecedent nor consequent. He is an isolated, definitive human datum, in stable equilibrium except for the buffets of the impinging forces that displace him in one direction or another.[2]

Thanks, Thorstein. Turns out my problem is that I was treating people like "a homogeneous globule of desire of happiness." (I wish I could write stuff like that.) Professor Veblen actually understates the problem.

Not only are we not "lightning calculators"; we actually refuse to use new information when we have entrenched beliefs. Psychologists have consistently shown that virtually everyone falls prey to "confirmation bias," a propensity to believe evidence in support of prior beliefs and to reject evidence that contradicts these beliefs. In other words, if you think an increase in the minimum wage won't destroy any jobs, then hard data I present to you that say otherwise will just look self-interested. You'll question my *motives* sooner than your own *beliefs*. On politically contentious topics, the cognitive scientists Hugo Mercier and Dan Sperber call this "myside bias."[3] They show in their research that people are remarkably good at finding the weaknesses in others' arguments but terrible at seeing the weaknesses in their own.

So if facts don't matter to most people, if their minds are made up in advance and they are immune to evidence, how can we ever come together on any issue? It seems that we will never see one another's arguments as worthy of consideration, making my quest in this book—to end the culture of contempt—a quixotic one at best.

Uri Hasson is a professor in the Psychology Department and the Neuroscience Institute at Princeton University. He runs the Hasson Lab, a cognitive neuroscience research group that spends its days studying brain images produced by a functional magnetic resonance imaging (fMRI) machine. By examining these images, Hasson and his colleagues are able to see the changes that occur in brain activity in the course of natural verbal communication. "In my lab in Princeton, we bring people to the fMRI scanner and we scan their brains while they are either telling or listening to real-life stories," he explains in a TED Talk describing his research.[4]

When telling or listening to the story, Hasson studies what each participant's brain activity looks like. "We start to scan their brains before the story starts, when they're simply lying in the dark and waiting for the story to begin," he says. These scans show that the individuals' patterns of brain activity are highly dissimilar and not in sync. "However, immediately as the story is starting, something amazing is happening," he says. The listener engages with the story, and suddenly his or her brain waves lock into a common pattern with the storyteller's. "It's a clear and dramatic correlation. The more listeners understand what the speaker is saying, the more closely their brain responses mirror the speaker's brain responses."[5]

This seemingly miraculous effect is "neural entrainment" or "brain-to-brain coupling."[6]

You may wonder: Are the brains just latching on to the speech patterns and language sounds rather than the actual substance of what is being said? Hasson tested this by exposing Russian and English speakers to the same story in their native languages, to see if the brain patterns depended on the language as opposed to the story. He found the same pattern.

Further, when the speaker and the listener were speaking the same language, he says, "The coupling was widespread across all different levels of the brain's network, from low-level processing of auditory information to higher functions." In fact, Hasson's studies showed that if the listener was drawn deeply into the story, his or her brain would actually get ahead of the narrative being shared—anticipating and actively predicting the speaker's upcoming utterances. "It's that feeling you get that you just click with someone. You can finish their sentences," he says.

When people ask, "Are you on my wavelength?" they usually mean it as a metaphor. Uri Hasson's brain imaging shows that this isn't just a metaphor; it's a real physiological phenomenon. You can literally get on the same wavelength as other people by telling a story. The fact that our brain activity moves in lockstep during storytelling is one of the best secrets to deeply understanding others. Unifying leaders, take note. Start your next speech with a personal story.

Advances in brain science are proving what people intuitively know, which apparently is beaten out of us as professional economists: stories bring people together. They possess the power to unite.

If you look at how people have tried to convince others of a moral position throughout history, you'll see that it's almost always been through the telling of human stories. Imagine Jesus telling his followers, "According to the latest surveys, priests and Levites are 42.3 percent less likely than Samaritans to help travelers on the road from Jerusalem to Jericho—on which, violent crime has increased significantly in the last decade." (This would have occurred shortly after he finished his PhD at Galilee State University.) He made the point with considerably more force with the parable of the Good Samaritan.

All the world's great religions feature stories of people in epic struggles. The ancient myths of the Greeks and the Romans are collections of moral tales. The Bhagavad Gita, the holiest book in Hinduism, is part of the Mahabharata, an epic drama of war. The Hebrew Bible is filled with exciting stories we all know, from the parting of the Red Sea to Jonah and the Whale. What the authors of these holy books knew thousands of years ago is being confirmed by neuroscientists like Uri Hasson with brain scans today. If you want people to learn something and remember it, put it in a story about people.

Thus it turns out that, just maybe, my effort to bring people together who disagree isn't an exercise in futility after all. I was just doing it wrong, relying on cold facts instead of human stories. When we tell stories, our brains unite, giving us the chance to at least understand one another, whether we ultimately agree or disagree. We can break down prejudice and division—we can defeat myside bias and induce openness, if not agreement—two brains at a time.

Brain-to-brain coupling isn't the only way that stories create human understanding. Another is through the strange effect of oxytocin, the "love molecule." Oxytocin is a hormone synthesized in the brain's hypothalamus; it makes us feel bonded to others. It leads mates to feel a special love for each other, allowing us to join some other species—such as shingleback skinks, French angelfish, and Atlantic puffins—in mating for life. ("I promise to be as faithful to you as a shingleback skink.")

It is even more powerful for bonding parents with their offspring. Maybe it seems obvious to you that people would naturally bond to their kids. But think about it. Babies give you plenty of reasons not to like them. (Remember Saint Augustine's denunciation of babies?) They can't do any work, they keep you up at night, and they scream like tyrants when they don't get what they want.

When my wife and I were expecting our first child, I actually had an odd little paranoid thought. *Am I going to really love him?* But when I held him for the very first time in the moments after he was born, and looked into his little eyes, something popped inside my head. I could almost feel it. What was it? It was oxytocin. My brain had released the love molecule, and I felt a connection to my son to the point where I would gladly die for him. I experienced the exact same sensation two years later, when our second son was born.

A few years after that, Ester and I decided to adopt a little girl, and I wondered, *Was the experience I had with my sons a biological connection? Would I feel the same connection with my adopted child?* Then I went to pick her up from an orphanage in China. She was a year and a half old. They called my name, I went into a room, and a nurse plopped a disoriented toddler I had never met into my arms. She grabbed my shirt with her little fists and stared up at me with her little eyes, and—

pop!—it happened again. Oxytocin. I could have sworn in that moment that we had been together forever, and we're still inseparable, fifteen years later.

By the way, don't take any of this as the case for some sort of material, earthbound concept of life. Some people think all our reactions and feelings are purely biological; I'm not one of them. In my daily prayers, I give thanks for things like oxytocin, which I consider a gift, not merely an adaptation of nature that kept me from leaving my baby out in the backyard overnight.

Baseline oxytocin levels are usually near zero, until some sort of stimulus causes its release into the brain and the bloodstream, where it has a half-life of about 3.5 minutes. This makes it a great molecule for scientific experiments. After it is released, changes in oxytocin levels in the brain can be measured in the blood, which means researchers can determine changes in our oxytocin levels with a simple blood test.

Dr. Paul Zak is an economist who runs experiments that do just that. The director of the Center for Neuroeconomics Studies at Claremont Graduate University, he studies the neuroscience of human connection and how stories actually change brain chemistry and allow us to achieve greater unity with one another. The key to unity, he tells me, is oxytocin.

"We're constantly balancing the appropriate fear of

being around strangers with the desire to interact with them, and so oxytocin helps maintain that balance," Zak tells me. "We have an underlying neurophysiology of human connection, of reciprocity, of cooperation," and by helping keep us calm and anxiety-free, oxytocin facilitates the kind of relational unity we so deeply desire.

"When the brain synthesizes oxytocin, people are more trustworthy, generous, charitable, and compassionate," he says. He has studied the release of oxytocin during religious rituals, folk dances, weddings, and even during a traditional war dance by indigenous people in a rain forest in Papua New Guinea. He has also studied it in his Southern California lab, where he pays test subjects about twenty dollars to sit in a chair and listen to a story while he sticks needles in their arms to obtain vials of blood, which he uses to measure the chemical changes produced by their brains.

Here is one story Zak shares with his test subjects: a short video shows a father talking to the camera while his two-year-old son, Ben, plays happily in the background.[7]

"Ben's dying," the father says.

He explains that the little boy, a patient at St. Jude Children's Research Hospital, has an inoperable brain cancer. He's just completed chemotherapy, which has temporarily beaten back his tumor, so he is running around and giggling like a normal child. But, his father explains, his cancer will soon come back with a vengeance and kill him. The happy little boy doesn't know that the tumor will take his life in a matter of months. Ben's father's voice begins to break as he explains how difficult it is to be joyful around Ben because he knows what is coming:

> For now, we've got Ben the way you see him . . . a playful, cheerful, happy kid. At some point, his tumor will begin to grow again, and it's a point where all of our known medicines stop working.
>
> There are no words to describe how it feels to know that your time is limited. There are no words.
>
> I look at his face and I see him smiling and running around and playing like a normal kid. And I think if he can do that, so can I. So, for now, I'm going to put on my smile, too. And I'm going to keep right on going with that boy, until he takes his last breath.

I'm sure you felt distress and empathy for Ben and his dad as you read this story. The impact is even more powerful when you watch the video and actually see Ben playing and his dad speaking. They are not actors.

Ben was a real boy with cancer, who has now died, and the father really is his father.

The reason we feel that way is that, as we hear that story about Ben, our brains release oxytocin, inducing a deep emotional understanding of Ben and his dad. It immediately made me think of my own kids when they were little, and my greatest fear, which was (and is) harm coming to one of them. "After [test subjects] watched the video, we had them rate their feelings and took blood before and after to measure oxytocin," Zak says.[8] "The change in oxytocin predicted their feelings of empathy. It's empathy that makes us connect to other people. It's empathy that makes us help other people."

To measure the behavioral impact of oxytocin, Zak gave the test subjects an opportunity to donate part of the money they earned for participating in the study to a childhood cancer charity. "When people watch Ben's story in the lab—and they both maintain attention to the story and release oxytocin—nearly all of these individuals donate a portion of their earnings from the experiment," Zak says.[9] Indeed, the more oxytocin the brain produced, the more likely the test subjects were to donate. He also found that "those who donated after watching Ben's story had more empathic concern for other people and were happier than those who did not donate money." Later, he reran the experiment using fMRI machines like the ones used by Uri Hasson. He found that the brain regions most active were the ones rich in oxytocin receptors that make us feel empathy.

The video of Ben and his father that Zak shows his test subjects is taken from a fund-raising video for St. Jude Children's Research Hospital. The test subjects can't help Ben—he has already passed away—but his story produces oxytocin in their brains, which elicits empathy for Ben and makes them want to do something to help others. In another experiment, Zak showed study participants sixteen public service ads from the United Kingdom that were produced by charities on topics such as smoking, speeding, drinking and driving, and global warming.[10] Half of the participants received synthetic oxytocin through a nasal inhaler, while the other half received a placebo. He found that those who received oxytocin donated to 57 percent more of the featured charities and donated 56 percent more money than the participants who received the placebo. "Those who received oxytocin also reported more emotional transportation into the world depicted in the ad," he says, and "said they were less likely to engage in the dangerous behaviors shown in the ads."

Oxytocin is one of the means by which the human race has continued to exist. It bonds us to our romantic partners. It bonds us to our children and other loved ones who are family members. It also bonds us, in lower concentrations, to our friends, and even to strangers—when they have a story we can relate to. When you tell somebody—even a stranger—a story about yourself that he can relate to, that relating induces people to produce oxytocin, which makes the person literally feel a bit of love for you. In the same way, you can love strangers a little more by listening to their stories. This is deep understanding.

Learning these facts about the power of human stories has helped me understand better my day-to-day work. Until a decade ago, I performed research on the behavioral economics of philanthropy, and even wrote a textbook on nonprofit management. I specialized in collecting and analyzing data on people's charitable giving. I could tell you how much people gave, and to what, and how different cultural and policy levers would change these things.

However, I had never looked anyone in the eye and asked the person for a contribution. Then I took over the presidency of a large nonprofit organization that is totally reliant on voluntary donations—tens of millions of dollars a year. I was a recognized scholar in the subject of charity, but was in a complete panic because I didn't know how to ask people for money. Basically, I was like the world's leading sports statistician suddenly facing a major-league pitcher. All the data in the world were not going to slow down that fastball.

My brother helped me get the hang of it. He is a specialist in the practice (not the theory) of fund-raising. He writes practical books and has a popular blog on the subject, and has helped raise billions for client organizations, from CARE International to the Salvation Army. His advice was to remember this one little inequality: 1>10,000,000. Maybe you're thinking my brother is really bad at math. Here's what he meant: When you are talking about people, ten million is a statistic; one person is a story, and stories win when you are trying to get people to support a cause.

Did you know that 180,000 children in sub-Saharan Africa die each year because they don't have clean drinking water?[11] That number sounds pretty bad, but it produces little if any human empathy per se. What if I introduce you to a little boy named Joey who lives in Tanzania? Joey has big, dark eyes and a distended belly. He looks right at you as a narrator explains, "This is Joey. Joey doesn't have access to safe drinking water. He drinks dirty water, which has given him parasites, and he may die of a waterborne illness, as have so many of his friends." No longer is the issue of clean drinking water an abstraction, difficult to relate to or fully comprehend. Now you *understand* the problem!

That is a fund-raising appeal that works because seeing Joey stimulates oxytocin in our brains. We feel neurological unity with him, we understand his plight at the human level, and we want to do something. We don't feel unity with the number 180,000. But we do feel unity with a child who is suffering, because that's how we're wired. We feel human love for people, not statistics.

It's not just charities that have come to understand this. For-profit marketers have, too. Remember the Pillsbury Doughboy, the Kool-Aid man (who crashed through the wall and said, "Oh, yeah!"), and the M&M guys? Those characters are actually the stuff of nightmares, when you think about it. ("Help me! My candy came to life!") And yet they sell product due to something called brand anthropomorphization, in which inanimate objects become relatable when they're given a human story.

This is important for fund-raising and brand marketing, but it's also important for being effective leaders and uniting society. Human stories do that by fostering a deep understanding of others. Brain science tells us we are made to bond to other people. We are wired for stories, and we're wired for relationships. Therefore, if we want to unite the country, we know what we each need to do: give people more oxytocin and more brain-to-brain coupling. Tell more stories.

When human stories are present, good things happen. But the opposite is also true: a storyless person disappears. In ancient Rome, a punishment worse than death for a criminal was *damnatio memoriae*, or "condemnation of memory," in which all traces of the person would be expunged, down to chipping their faces off statues.[12] More recently, in the Soviet Union, history books were changed routinely by the government to make stories about individuals who were out of official favor evaporate from memory, just as they were made physically to disappear.

As every tyrant knows, dehumanization—or as social scientists sometimes call it, deindividuation—destroys empathy and compassion and makes possible the most horrific predations. Stalin famously declared, "When one man dies, it's a tragedy. When thousands die, it's statistics."[13] Kill one person, go to jail; tens of millions, go to Yalta. He systematically eradicated an entire class of people, affluent peasant landowners known as Kulaks. According to Stanford historian Norman Naimark, this mass murder was preceded by a campaign of dehumanization, in which the Kulaks were depicted as "'swine' [and] 'dogs' . . . they were 'scum,' 'vermin,' 'filth,' and 'garbage' . . . [and] 'half animals.'" This dehumanization made their stories as people disappear and allowed them "to be cleansed, crushed and eliminated."[14] Millions were killed so that their lands could be seized by the Soviet regime.

Similarly, the Nazis eliminated the human stories of the Jews to enable the Holocaust. In 1940, Nazi propaganda minister Joseph Goebbels compared Jews to rats.[15] His most famous film for the German people featured images of rats, while the narrator declares: "Where rats appear, they bring ruin by destroying mankind's goods and foodstuffs. In this way, they spread disease, plague, leprosy, typhoid fever, cholera, dysentery, and so on. They are cunning, cowardly and cruel and are found mostly in large packs. Among the animals, they represent the rudiment of an insidious, underground destruction—just like the Jews among human beings." The Nazis depicted Jews as rats because they wanted to exterminate them—and to do that they had to dehumanize them, taking away their faces and the human stories of their lives, families, friends, and work.

The same thing happened during the Rwandan genocide, wherein the Hutus referred to the Tutsis as *inyenzi*, which means "cockroaches." As one Rwandan

newspaper explained on the twentieth anniversary
of the genocide, "Equating Tutsi with cockroaches
meant that few would think twice about killing and at-
tempting to exterminate something so vile, dirty and
sneaky. . . . And, in the end, from politician to the
ordinary farmer, Hutus united to get rid of the 'cockroaches,' working together to exterminate their Tutsi
friends, neighbors, co-workers and family members."[16]
During a hundred-day period in 1994, 70 percent of
the Tutsi population, approximately one million people, were slaughtered by their neighbors.

This process is not limited to foreign genocidal
maniacs. Dehumanization and deindividuation are the
sources of bigotry, discrimination, and the culture of
contempt in our own society. That is the story of slavery
in the United States, as well as the treatment of Native
Americans. On a much smaller scale today, dehumanization characterizes the rhetoric of leaders who treat
with contempt immigrants, poor people, or simply those
on the other political side.

Be on the lookout for dehumanization in everyday
life. You will start to see it. For example, perhaps your
favorite newspaper pundit refers to certain people as
pigs. The point is to destroy your empathy for the object
of his or her derision through dehumanization. Perhaps

that seems like no big deal, but make no mistake: You are being manipulated to hate a fellow human being.

When individuals are deindividuated by having their human stories taken away, they can be treated poorly. That's bad enough, but here's the really insidious thing: When we let *ourselves* be deindividuated, we behave worse as well. We see this effect all the time when otherwise decent people get caught up in an angry mob. This doesn't just refer to a riot or violent demonstration; it can even be a campus lecture or political town hall meeting where a crowd shouts down a speaker.

The French psychologist Gustave Le Bon was the world's leading expert in the psychology of deindividuated crowds. In his magisterial 1895 text *The Crowd: A Study of the Popular Mind,* he showed that individuals act differently in crowds than they do when they are alone.[17] People are mostly decent and humane when you get them one-on-one, but when you get them into a crowd, they can change very quickly. Le Bon found that crowds tend to have a lower cognitive ability and a lower moral threshold. Crowds, he argued, are inherently "unanimous, emotional and intellectually weak."[18] Think of a crowd kind of like a big, angry drunk—and act accordingly for your own safety.

Stacks of research confirm that deindividuation can

lower inhibitions against immoral behavior. In one of my favorite studies, researchers set up a bowl of candy for Halloween trick-or-treaters, told them to take just one piece, and then left them alone.[19] Some of the children were in anonymous groups, others were by themselves. When kids were part of a group, 60 percent took more than one piece of candy. When they were by themselves but not asked their names, 20 percent cheated. But when they were alone and asked their names, only 10 percent took more than they were allotted.

Other studies show that even the *illusion* of anonymity disinhibits people from dishonest behavior. One experiment found that students in a room with slightly dimmed lighting cheated more than those in a well-lit room, while another found that participants wearing sunglasses behaved more selfishly than those wearing clear glasses.[20] It is no coincidence that the New Testament warns us that "everyone who does evil hates the light and will not come into the light for fear that their deeds will be exposed. But whoever lives by the truth comes into the light, so that it may be seen plainly that what they have done has been done in the sight of God."[21]

I often reflect on how differently people act when they drive, encased in a car and thus anonymous, compared with the way they act when they walk on the street.

Imagine if another pedestrian inadvertently cut you off on the sidewalk. He'd apologize and you'd say, "No problem, have a good day." But in the car, you might honk and give him the finger. I imagine how great it would be if everyone had to have a bumper sticker with his or her name—and as a bonus, his or her house of worship or favorite charity. I'm a lot less likely to get flipped off by Larry Jones from Our Lady of Sorrows than some anonymous guy.

I have come to notice changes in my own behavior when I am anonymous, versus when people know me or something about me. In the most amusing example of this, I recently noticed a big behavioral change even when what people knew about me was false.

Several years ago, I was giving a guest lecture at Brigham Young University. BYU is the flagship university of the Church of Jesus Christ of Latter-day Saints (informally called the Mormons). I love visiting BYU, because the people there are unfailingly kind. They are also generous, frequently sending me home with a load of branded souvenirs for the entire family: T-shirts, hoodies, hats, mugs—you name it. (They are good at product placement.) On this particular trip, they gave me an especially nice gift—an Italian briefcase, with the university's name emblazoned across the front. When I got home, I showed it to my wife, and remarked what a lovely gift it was. Then I promptly put it in the closet and forgot about it, because I already had a briefcase.

A few months passed, and one day the handle on the briefcase I was carrying broke. I was irritated and complained to Ester about the shoddy workmanship. Her response was, "Well, why don't you go to the closet and get that BYU briefcase?" I hesitated. She smiled, and asked, "What's the matter? Are you worried people are going to think you're a Mormon?" No, I told her, but we're Catholics, so it feels a little like false advertising. She wasn't buying my excuses. "You know what?" she asked. "I think you're *afraid* people will think you're a Mormon."

There's an old joke: "My wife says I'm consumed with thoughts of vengeance, but I say . . . we'll just see about that." Since my life seems to be based on a series of corny jokes, that's what I said in response to the briefcase challenge issued by my wife: "We'll just see about that." I went to the closet, got out my BYU briefcase, filled it up with my stuff, and started carrying it around.

I travel a lot, and I spend a great deal of time in airports. I quickly noticed that people would look at my briefcase, and then look up at me, and I could tell that they were putting two and two together, thinking something like, *What a weird-looking guy, with his loud socks, skinny tie, bright orange wristwatch, and BYU briefcase. I've never seen an aging hipster Mormon before.* This gave me minor amusement at first, but I noticed it was having an effect on my behavior. No sooner had people started mistaking me for a Latter-day Saint than I started acting like I thought one would act. I began behaving more cheerfully and courteously than I ordinarily would—helping people with luggage, giving up my place in line, and generally being friendly. When I finished at the ticket counter, I would smile and say, "Have a nice day." It was like I was playing a bit part named Mormon Guy in a movie.

I not only behaved better; I also stopped doing certain things. On one trip, I was about to go into the airport Starbucks when I remembered, *Mormons aren't supposed to drink coffee.* I imagined a religious skeptic watching me put down my BYU briefcase to pay for my venti latte, and then telling his wife when he got home, "You know, those Mormons are a bunch of hypocrites. I saw one of them at the airport carrying a Starbucks latte. I knew it! When they think no one is paying attention, they drink coffee just like the rest of us!" I didn't want that. I had to protect their reputation. I drink coffee; they don't. I'm carrying their briefcase, so I don't drink coffee while doing so.

My briefcase told a story that prevented me from

acting anonymously. True, the story it gave me was not genuinely my own, but it humanized me nonetheless—and improved my behavior.

In Le Bon's time, a crowd was a physical phenomenon. Not anymore, necessarily. The most significant example today of negative deindividuation—a venue where stories are stripped away and bad behavior reigns supreme—is in social media. For starters, sites such as Twitter obscure the fullness of our human stories, eviscerating nuance and context. It is almost inevitable that when stories are reduced to just 280 characters, we jump to conclusions about others, resort to ad hominem attacks, and act as a mob against individuals. Social media doesn't just shorten our stories, though; by facilitating anonymity in a virtual world, it allows us to behave as though our stories are completely invisible to others.

The Internet is essentially a virtual crowd made up of billions of people. When people melt into the anonymity of this virtual community, they often behave abhorrently, as anyone who has been on Twitter or read the comments section of a major newspaper can attest. Read a news article called "I Love Puppies," and the fourth anonymous comment about the story will probably be something vulgar, racist, and hateful.

Unlike a physical crowd, moreover, a virtual crowd on social media has unlimited reach. The deindividuated mob can find you anywhere through your computer or smartphone. As a result, the rise of social media has scaled up our ability to express contempt and vitriol and to act as a deindividuated lumpen mass with astonishing efficiency.

Before you dismiss this as harmless, consider a 2014 article in the academic journal *Personality and Individual Differences*, titled "Trolls Just Want to Have Fun."[22] Three Canadian psychologists found that habitual Internet commenting is strongly correlated with dangerous personality pathologies. The total amount of time spent posting comments online correlated positively with sadism, psychopathy, and Machiavellianism. This was especially true for those who relished "trolling," the anonymous posting of negative and destructive comments. The participants who listed trolling as their favorite activity earned the highest scores on those unsavory psychological measures.

The evidence on online anonymity is alarming, although it could have its practical uses. When you're on a first date, slip in the question, "Do you have an anonymous Twitter account?" If the person says yes, say no to a second date. There is a much higher probability than average that he or she exhibits narcissistic sociopathy with low levels of empathy—not the characteristics you want in the mother or father of your children.

My personal view is that anonymity on the Internet is a net bad and should be actively discouraged by private companies and in personal behavior. Social media companies, as a matter of basic corporate responsibility and ultimately self-preservation (so their platforms are not hopelessly degraded), should require proof of real identity in order to hold an account and post.

For us as individuals, if the problem is deindividuation online, then the solution is reindividuation. If you are as appalled as I am by the coarsening of public discourse, then remove yourself from the angry crowd and reclaim your individual story. Repudiate anonymity and be yourself online. Make a commitment today to never be anonymous or say anything anonymously.

As you repudiate your own anonymity, also make a commitment never to engage with others when they are anonymous online. Social media companies might or might not ultimately require people to reveal their identities before participating, but even if they don't, you don't have to engage with people hiding behind anonymity. Never get into a Twitter feud with somebody whose name is TrumpLover2016 or BernieBro2020. That's not a real person, in terms of morals and behavior. Make a commitment to ignore the anonymous haters. Anonymity is a cancer that is wrecking our country, because it obliterates our ability to understand one another through authentic human stories.

Some will argue with me, saying that anonymous speech is an important tradition in a free society. Indeed it is, when there is the threat of a knock in the night from a jackbooted thug. But let's be realistic: We have succeeded spectacularly in protecting speech in America; criticism on social media is not physical harm by a mob. And Twitter is not exactly the *Federalist Papers*.

While you're at it, cut back on social media. There's a growing body of research that shows that excessive time spent on social media is associated with loneliness and depression.[23] Why? I have no doubt because we crave human contact, which means sharing our common humanity in the real world—not outlandish anonymous insults and (at best) the incomplete narratives of others' lives.

You can see that the evidence is clear. Though we may not ultimately agree on every issue, we can still come to understand one another. To understand others and help them understand us, we must make a human connection, and the way to do this is through stories.

Knowing this isn't easy for me. Remember, I'm an economist. We almost never tell human stories but rather work on data sets, finding "empirical regularities" that are supposed to illuminate the secrets of human behavior. But it's not just my toolkit that holds me back. Frankly, I don't have a lot of natural trust for storytelling, because it is so often used dishonestly in the media to eviscerate the truths contained in data.

I run a think tank full of experts who care deeply about policy and use data to show what's best for people and what isn't. Sometimes it's counterintuitive. Take, for instance, the problems with America's safety-net policies. For many years, the scholars at my institution—who believe in a government welfare system—have shown what they believe is overwhelming evidence that the safety-net programs designed in the 1960s tend to trap people in dependency, and thus hurt those they are intended to help. My colleagues advocate other welfare policies that improve the ability to earn a living without the harmful side effects.

And yet, when our scholars publish a study promoting reforms to the welfare system, it seems there is always a news story about the study that "refutes" it by profiling an individual who may be adversely affected by the change. I know this kind of story is more compelling than our data on thousands of faceless poor people. It is a classic case of 1>10,000,000. But it is also wrong. It would be like me saying, "Ten million kids lack access to clean water," and you retorting, "I disagree, because I know a kid named Joey who has plenty of clean water."

During a lot of my career, I resisted stories because I saw them as distortionary and manipulative, even dishonest. The right use of stories is that in which we employ them to motivate the truths in the data. Joey's story should move us to both alleviate his individual suffering *and* address the very real and urgent plight of millions of children around the world. Thus I need to find the stories in my work that help people relate emotionally to what my analysis is showing to be true.

Fine, you might be saying—but how? What do I do to find the stories in my work? For the answer to this, I love the words of Pope Francis in a sermon he delivered to the American Catholic bishops in his visit to the United States in 2013. He told them they should be "shepherds living with the smell of the sheep."[24] If you are doing work that helps others, you should spend time among the people you are working to help. You need to "smell like the sheep" if you want to learn the stories of people's lives. In virtually every case where people struggle with storytelling, it is because they are too far away from the subject of their work.

This observation has had a big impact on me. It's easy to talk about economic policy, or defense policy, or education policy, as somehow distant from real people.

That's the recipe for policies that sound good but don't work, or that feed pieties without actually helping others. A standard part of my work today involves getting into the public all the time to ask people their stories. Among other things, this has made me more politically independent and tolerant of alternate points of view, because I clearly see that no one has a lock on the right ideas when they are exposed to real lives.

However, it's not just other people's stories we need to seek out and share. You and I need to tell our own as well. The telling begins with the short story of your life's mission, the "why" behind what you do and what you believe, not just your political or other demographic identities. Can you tell me a story that states your life's purpose in twenty seconds or less? How about ten? Being able to do so will affect the way you behave and the way others behave toward you. If you want more unity with other people and you want to create more unity among those around you, you have to get comfortable telling your story, quickly and compellingly.

Here's a practical tip to start telling your story: write it down in twelve words or less. Sounds impossible, right? There is a legend that the great novelist Ernest Hemingway once made a bet with a friend that he could craft an entire story in *six* words. His friend took the bet, because he knew that no one could write a story in six words that would have any emotional impact or importance at all. Hemingway pulled out a piece of paper and wrote down these six words:

"For sale: baby shoes, never worn."

We might not all be Hemingways, but we can all tell a succinct story about ourselves. So, put down this book and write out your twelve-word story. By doing so, you'll be able to make a human connection with others. Once you have your story in twelve words so that you understand it yourself, start sharing it with other people, so they understand *you*.

By the way, want to know mine? "A lucky man, dedicated to lifting others up and bringing them together."

Finally—no cowbell.

Chapter 7
Is Competition Our Problem?

I started to suspect the American competitive spirit was in trouble when they banned dodgeball.

In March 2013, the Windham, New Hampshire, school board voted 4–1 to get rid of the game in the schools.[1] It had already been banned by school districts around the country. The Windham school board's vice chair explained the decision in the context of the tragic Sandy Hook school shooting, which had recently left twenty children dead, saying, "We live in a world where 20 babies were slaughtered. We need to take violence out of our schools and not teach it."[2]

In truth, dodgeball (which, for readers deprived of its joys as children, involves throwing balls as hard as possible at other kids to get them "out") is one of the worst memories of my generally happy childhood. Back in fourth grade, a kid named Donald with a wicked arm made a point of throwing the ball at my face, over and over. The gym teacher, a nasty piece of work with a whistle, egged him on. Not that I'm bitter.

But I digress. The attack on dodgeball seemed to me more philosophical than practical, especially given that a 1992 article in the *Journal of Physical Education, Recreation & Dance* titled "The Physical Education Hall of Shame" started the anti-dodgeball trend by marking it for eradication alongside other competitive games such as red rover, tag, duck duck goose, and (I kid you not) musical chairs.[3] Getting rid of dodgeball is part of a larger trend against head-to-head competitive activities.

The idea that competitive games are deleterious comes from worries about self-esteem, of course, but there is another motivation with which you might agree: a desire to teach cooperation. There is a widespread belief that when people compete, they become unnecessarily adversarial, hampering the development of cooperative sentiments and skills. This leads young people to see the world as "us versus them," with all of the attendant conflicts we would prefer to avoid. According to the Indian philosopher Jiddu Krishnamurti, "Real learning comes about when the competitive spirit has ceased."[4]

All this is rooted in what might seem to you the most straightforward of all truths: competition might be inevitable in many areas, but it is never better than a second-best solution. Harmonious cooperation should be the true objective in our interactions with one another. As Pope Francis declared in a 2017 sermon in Rome, "communion must be victorious over competition."[5]

And where could this be truer than in the world of ideas? Shouldn't cooperation be our goal—not competition—if we are to love our enemies?

Women's hockey is a fairly new sport in elite international competition. It was first played in the winter Olympics in just 1998. But since its inclusion, two teams have utterly dominated: the United States and Canada. In fact, these two teams have played each other for the gold medal in every Olympics since the sport's first appearance in the quadrennial games. Canada has won four times; the US, twice. Similarly, the two teams have played each other in every world championship since 1990 (Canada 10, United States 8).

That's great, if you're a fan of U.S. or Canadian women's hockey, right?

Wrong. It's not great; it's incredibly boring. Think about it: Who wants to watch a sports league with only two competitive teams? At the 2010 Vancouver Olympics, the United States and Canada outscored all other nations by a combined tally of 88–4. It was pitiful to watch Canada massacre Slovakia 18–0 and the United States annihilate Russia 13–0. Some began asking whether a sport so dominated by just two countries even belonged at the Olympics. International Olympic Committee president Jacques Rogge announced that "we cannot continue without improvement" among other countries.[6] The lack of serious competition posed an existential threat to the sport.

Fortunately, at the 2018 Pyeongchang Games, the gap between North America and the rest of the world began to close. The United States and Canada still dominated, but they outscored their opponents by a far more competitive 35–10. The United States defeated Russia by only 5 goals, not 13. No team scored more than 8 goals in a game. The progress was substantial enough that the International Ice Hockey Federation announced it was recommending going from eight teams to ten for the 2022 Beijing Winter Games.

This is a paradox, isn't it? We want our team to win, so it stands to reason that we should hope for lousy competition. Yet we don't: We want our side to defeat *worthy opponents*. Why? Because only in the face of quality competitors can the team demonstrate its excellence. Only where there is fierce competition are people interested in watching the game.

This leads us to the first truth of competition: it

fosters and sustains excellence. This is why great competitors seek out, and even require, worthy opponents. It is mutual excellence that makes competition fierce, captivating to watch, and even beautiful. (Indeed, once I saw my father-in-law, an avid cycling fan, weep at the end of a stage of the Tour de France, so beautiful was the photo finish.)

Does an embrace of fierce competition mean we want to win by any means necessary? Not at all. Take the teams Real Madrid and FC Barcelona, two of the greatest soccer clubs in the world and bitter rivals going back to the 1930s. Their matches are some of the most-followed regular sporting events in the world; indeed, all over Spain and Latin America (and in my house in Maryland), life practically stops when they play. Every soccer fan has an opinion on this rivalry, which has strong political dimensions in a country riven by separatism and struggling with a history of political repression. Fans of each club would pay good money to see their side win. But what happens if Barcelona's star player goes down with a blown-out knee? Do Madrid's fans cheer his season-ending injury? No, they mostly fall silent. Why? Because Madrid fans want to beat Barcelona through excellence, not injury—and vice versa. They don't want there to be any question as to which team is better.

Even less would we want our team to win by cheating. If the New York Yankees sabotaged the Boston Red Sox team bus on the way to Yankee Stadium, it would be the source of no pride or enjoyment at all for true New York fans. The reason is that this is exactly the opposite of true competition; it is *shutting competition down*. True competition requires rules and fair play, and the goal is to win within those rules. To break those rules and shut competition down is to both delegitimize victory and deprive ourselves of the enjoyment of excellence.

After the Sochi Winter Olympics in 2014, sports fans were outraged when they learned that Russia had engaged in what Olympic officials declared was "the systemic manipulation of the anti-doping rules."[7] It turns out that the FSB (the successor to the KGB) had built a secret laboratory in a storage room adjacent to the one where urine samples from athletes were kept. Samples were passed through a hidden hole in the wall, and Russian spies took the bottles, which were designed with special anti-tampering caps, and found a way to replace the tainted samples with untainted urine without breaking the caps. About a hundred tainted samples were made to "disappear" in this way. According to the IOC, one-third of Russia's thirty-three medals were awarded to athletes whose samples were cleansed. The result?

The entire Russian squad was banned from competition at the 2018 Pyeongchang Games. Rightly so, as far as everyone I know is concerned.

Nothing disgusts sports fans—although not post-Soviet politicians, apparently—more than a cheating scandal. There's a reason why Nike sells shoes with the motto "Just do it," not "Cheat to win."

When one team is accused of breaking the rules, fans of competing teams are outraged. Witness the outpouring of vitriol directed at the New England Patriots in 2015. The team was accused of deflating footballs in order to gain an edge over the Indianapolis Colts in the AFC Championship Game—a game the Patriots won 45–7. The criticism they faced for their alleged subterfuge came fast and furious. THE LESSON: CHEATERS DO WIN, declared the *Indianapolis Star*.[8] BREAKING, BENDING RULES IS PATS' WAY, trumpeted the *New York Post*.[9]

However, observe the defense that Patriots fans made of their team. No one said, "Hey, suckers, we cheated and won. That makes us real winners!" They took their cue from team owner Robert Kraft, vehemently denying that any cheating ever happened, and outraged that anyone would accuse them of any such thing.[10] No one likes a cheat. Perhaps more significant, no one wants to be thought of as a cheat.

We thus arrive at the second truth about competition:

It requires rules in order to properly function. Rules in sports—clear and impartial—provide needed structure and make things fair. Breaking the rules, then, is the same as electing *not to compete.*

However, while rules provide structure and an even playing field for competition, they do not enforce themselves. This means that rules-based competition first requires us to come together around voluntarily agreed-upon principles. Red Sox and Yankee fans don't see eye to eye on much, especially with a few beers in them, but both will tell you a pitch down the middle is a strike, a pitch into the stands is a ball, and a pitch at a batter's head is grounds for ejection. If the Yankees applied one set of rules to themselves but enforced a different set of rules for their opponents, genuine competition would be impossible. If the Yankees manager asserted that in Yankee Stadium, the home team gets four outs in an inning, even the most rabid Yankees fan would say he's nuts.

That's the third truth: True competition requires voluntary cooperation with the rules. Mutually agreed-upon (and enforced) rules and principles grant legitimacy to the competitive process, and they keep us from descending into chaos.

Competing within mutually agreed-upon boundaries

also serves another important purpose. It bonds us all together around those things we mutually admire and care about: the beauty and excitement of sport; the consistent excellence of world-class athletes; and the feeling of achievement that comes from winning fair and square. I love the Seattle Seahawks, because I grew up in Seattle. My son roots for the Washington Redskins, because he grew up outside Washington, DC. We watch them play each other and we each hope our team wins. But we both love the competition, and watching the game together brings us closer as father and son.

Notice that sports fans are drawn to one another, and even nonfans use sports to talk to people they don't know. When I'm at a dinner put together by my wife and her friends, and I don't know the other husbands, I often find myself talking about sports. It's not that football is what I care about the most; in truth, I can't believe it when I hear myself say something like "Russell Wilson is looking pretty strong this year." It's just that I want a point of common ground with people with whom I'm going to spend a few hours.

That's the fourth truth: Competition, properly understood and practiced, unites people.

Let's briefly summarize a few conclusions about competition, as learned from the world of sports:

- Competition breeds excellence. Therefore, in order to sustain excellence and retain the interest of fans, teams must face worthy opponents.

- True competition in sports requires rules. Thus, winning by cheating is not a form of competition; it is a way to *shut down* competition.

- Mutual recognition of the rules and compliance with them is a form of cooperation. In this way, competition and cooperation are symbiotic, not mutually exclusive.

- Athletic competition, which follows the first three truths, unifies people through an admiration for athletic excellence, voluntary agreement on the rules, and the shared experience of watching the game.

In sports, it's clear that competition is great. What about in economics? That's a harder one for a lot of people to get their minds around. Lots of people have rejected the idea that economic competition is good, because, well, it feels a little too much like dodgeball. Wouldn't cooperation be better?

Back in the 1980s, the fast food chain Wendy's ran a famous TV ad depicting a fashion show in the old Soviet

Union.[11] As the show's emcee declares, in a thick Russian accent, "Day wear!" a Russian woman struts across the catwalk wearing a drab, proletarian cloth dress. "Very nice," says the announcer. Next up? "Evening wear!" The same woman struts across the catwalk in the exact same dress—but holding a flashlight. Swim wear? Same woman, same dress—this time holding a beach ball. The tagline: "Having no choice is no fun."

But this goes beyond clever commercials. In economics, competition leads to higher quality and lower prices for consumers. Everybody knows this, and it's the reason we break up monopolies and prohibit collusion. As obvious as this may sound to every reader of this book, however, it was definitely *not* obvious to people only a couple of centuries ago. The cultural revolution that was free enterprise brought this insight to individuals all over the world—especially in the United States—as companies competed for customers in quality and prices in relatively free markets. This competition significantly raised living standards, and ensured the ability of ordinary people to get ahead.

Economists of all political stripes have found that it is economic competition—bounded by appropriate guardrails (more on that in a moment)—that led to the incredible explosion in worldwide prosperity that began in 1970. Indeed, the percentage of the population living in starvation-level poverty around the world has fallen by more than four-fifths over the last fifty years.[12] This amounts to some two billion people lifted from extreme poverty due to the global spread of free enterprise. No other economic system has a remotely similar track record. This is not a political statement; quite the contrary. As no less an avowed progressive than President Barack Obama put it in a 2015 public conversation we had together at Georgetown University, the "free market is the greatest producer of wealth in history—it has lifted billions of people out of poverty."[13]

The first reason competition brings out all this benefit is because, once again, it foments excellence. Maybe like me, you use an Apple computer. It is a beautiful, well-functioning product. I am writing this book on a Mac laptop—writing anyplace I want, whether it's in an airplane, a coffee shop, or sitting in my office.

What keeps Apple products so good, year after year? Market competition, of course. Apple has tons of competitors, and they want people like me to stay loyal to their products. They keep my loyalty through a combination of high quality and extraordinary innovation that makes my life easier each day. Apple wants to beat the competition, to prosper as a great company with products people love.

It's not just about money. Here are the words of

Apple's CEO, Tim Cook, when asked about his competitors: "Honestly, we'll compete with everybody. I love competition. As long as people invent their own stuff, I love competition."[14]

I believe he means it. You can be cynical about this if you want. I'm not. In my line of work, I meet a lot of leaders of great companies. They almost all talk like this. They *love* competition, because they love improvement and winning against worthy market opponents. They love to earn their success. So while you might think that deep in Coca-Cola headquarters they are plotting to wipe out Pepsi, the truth is that they know it's Pepsi that keeps them on their toes. If Pepsi folds, it may temporarily increase their market share, but it will make them weaker in the long run. If they put out a commercial saying Pepsi will poison you, it would probably make millions of people—who, like me, can't tell the difference between Pepsi and Coke—avoid their own products as well.

Does every CEO love competition? No—only the ones who are great competitors themselves. The ones who hate competition are the mediocre leaders and mediocre companies that prefer to skate through without improvement. These are the ones who try to bend the rules in their favor, get special deals from the tax system, or break the law.

Just like sports, free-market competition requires rules so that competitors don't take advantage of one another. Corporate cronyism, monopoly, and corruption make us justifiably angry. We pass laws and regulate these things (though not as well as we should) so the game isn't fixed in favor of the fat cats, and against the consumers and smaller competitors. We know intuitively that when huge corporations lobby for regulations that benefit them and hurt their little competitors, when CEOs bribe government officials, or when a company dominates an industry so thoroughly as to make entry impossible, *it's not competition*. That is *shutting competition down.*

Furthermore, the fact that people in the economy believe in and generally submit to the rules of fair competition reveals the importance of cooperation. And it's a deeply American kind of cooperation at that. There's an old Russian saying, "If you pay your taxes, you're cheating your family." It's impossible to imagine that as an expression in the United States. I know lots of Americans who think individual and corporate taxes are too high, but I personally know no one who thinks tax evasion is a decent and moral thing to do. I am well aware that cheating goes on in the United States, but even when people bend the rules, they generally make excuses or hide their behavior, especially around those whom they respect. As a sex worker once proudly told the *New York Times Magazine*, "Strippers pay their taxes."[15]

The knock-on effect of seeing the benefits of economic competition and accepting rules of fair play is that Americans generally trust and admire people who legitimately succeed, even those who become wealthy. As one 2013 poll from the Pew Research Center found, 88 percent of Americans said they admired people who get rich by working hard.[16] Indeed, America's nearly universal admiration for earned success distinguishes this country from most other countries. This shouldn't come as a surprise, though: 73 percent of Americans believe working hard is important for getting ahead in life, 23 percentage points more than the global median.[17]

It is an incredible historical achievement that people of different classes can live together with a common sense of national purpose, with no realistic threat of the class violence seen over so much of history and in so many parts of the world still today. In 1835, Alexis de Tocqueville, commenting on the attitudes of Americans toward the wealthy, observed, "In the United States, the people have no hatred for the elevated classes of society," and that "they do not fear great talents."[18] For the almost two hundred years since the publication of *Democracy in America*, the United States has eschewed, as Tocqueville described it, the "envy that animates the lower classes . . . against the upper."[19]

What Americans *do* resent is not that others prosper per se, but that others prosper by *gaming the system*—further evidence that true competition, as we understand it, requires cooperation with the rules of fair play.

What should the rules of economic competition be? That's where things start to get complicated. Some people think they should be strong and intrusive, with a lot of regulations and laws, even if this comes at a high cost. Others favor a light touch, relying more on private morality, even if it means some rule-breaking slips through. But the fact that we disagree on the specifics (though not the necessity) of rules of economic competition is a reality that leads me to the most important and beneficial kind of competition: the *competition of ideas*. That means different points of view on all sorts of issues, competing in the arena of ideas in a vigorous, but respectful, democratic fashion.

I know this is still hard for some people to accept, because, hey, if I'm right and you're wrong, we don't need both sides of an issue, right? That basically sums up our political discourse in America today.

But it's wrong. John Stuart Mill explained it best in

1848 when he wrote in his *Principles of Political Economy*, "It is hardly possible to overrate the value . . . of placing human beings in contact with persons dissimilar to themselves, and with modes of thought and action unlike those with which they are familiar. . . . Such communication has always been, and is peculiarly in the present age, one of the primary sources of progress."[20] In a free society, both new and old ideas interact in the public square, allowing us to improve as individuals and as a nation. Following Mill, that competition of ideas is a true moral good. It strengthens America's free society by creating choice in the democratic process, fostering policy innovation, and providing a peaceful outlet for citizen discontent.

In other words, Mill believed that to develop excellent ideas, we need competing ideas. That is why it is so dangerous when powerful actors work not to win the competition of ideas, but instead to shut it down—by narrowing acceptable discourse, squashing protest, silencing opposing viewpoints, and saying people of opposing opinions are stupid or evil.

That is what is happening in our politics today, when one 2016 presidential candidate accuses the other of promoting the policy preferences of "a paranoid fringe" and the other's rejoinder is to call the first candidate a criminal and "the worst (and biggest) loser of all time."[21] In neither case is there any engagement with the actual substance of the policies in question. Rather, these are both attempts to shut the competition of ideas down by delegitimizing an ideological opponent—and his or her supporters—as out of touch, deviant, or incompetent.

This is not just unfair. It is unwise, because competition propels progress. We need Republicans and Democrats to argue fiercely over the best ways to combat poverty, reduce dependency, and give more Americans the opportunity to achieve the happiness of earned success. We need conservatives and liberals to fight vigorously over the best ways to protect our national security while also preserving our individual liberties. We need the left and the right to debate energetically the best ways to improve education so that the next generation has the tools to pursue and achieve the American Dream.

We all want a safer, fairer, more prosperous country. We just disagree on how to achieve that aim. We need a passionate competition of ideas so that each side refines its solutions, becomes more innovative, and therefore the best ideas rise to the top. Shutting down the competition of ideas makes it harder to achieve our common moral goals.

The benefits of idea competition go beyond national excellence—they affect personal excellence. The Proverbs teach us that "as iron sharpens iron, so one person sharpens another."[22] Edmund Burke wrote, "He that wrestles with us strengthens our nerves, and sharpens our skill. Our antagonist is our helper."[23] Modern research confirms this contention. As scholars at the University of Pennsylvania have found across a group of some 1,600 leaders, "boundary spanning"—bridging ideological divides—helps us understand the views of those who disagree with us while simultaneously improving our ability to defend our own beliefs.[24]

Great CEOs know this. They don't surround themselves with sycophants and yes-men who tell them whatever they already think is right. In the best of cases, such a practice lowers performance, because there are fewer ideas in the mix; it explains why one study of CEOs finds they tend to see falling performance in the second half of their tenures. They start relying too much on their own judgment as opposed to the ideas of others.[25] In the worst cases, it leads to disasters that could be averted with a little critical feedback. The *Harvard Business Review* has dispensed this simple piece of advice: "Hire people who disagree with you."[26]

This is not just about leaders, however. Want to be a more persuasive person? To make sure your ideas are well grounded and you don't get wiped out in a debate? The way to do it is *not* to hang around where everyone agrees, your ideas are never challenged, and people who disagree with you are shouted down. Nor to watch exclusively a television channel that tells you only what you already know and that the other side are knaves and fools. Nor to curate your social media in such a way that it only feeds your outrage about your opponents. These things will make your ideas weak and mediocre, not strong and secure.

It is especially true that we need a vigorous competition in our universities—the nation's factories of ideas. This is where the benefits are the greatest and where we can least afford conformity or mediocrity, because it is where young leaders for our future are being formed.

Universities are like sports camps, dedicated to making the best athletes in the world. Go to an Olympic training facility, and what do you see? Athletes subject to brutal resistance, intense competition, and almost unbearable discomfort. My kids all played sports. The training they all faced was grueling, and as a parent, it was agonizing to watch. But the payoff was clear when they won a championship, as my daughter did in gymnastics and my son did in cycling.

It was even clear when they lost. My oldest son was less of an athlete than the other two. He ran cross-country for four years in high school, and almost always came in dead last. In his senior year, he was made captain of the team, not for his prowess but his dogged determination, which is another aspect of excellence learned from competition. It was this learned skill that he wrote about in his entrance essay for college.

Imagine if the U.S. Olympic Team decided that team sports were bad for self-esteem, that painful training to improve skills was harmful, and that being exposed to competitors would make the athletes feel unsafe. Ridiculous, of course. Unfortunately, in too many cases today, we are doing something akin to this in universities, and a new generation of American leaders is being taught that a competition of ideas is dangerous and unacceptable; that it is acceptable to shut down the competition if the other side's ideas make students uncomfortable.

This trend doesn't just defy the principles of excellence; it also flies in the face of one of the great intellectual and moral epiphanies of our time—that human diversity is beneficial *per se*. It has become conventional wisdom that being around those unlike ourselves makes us better people—and more productive, to boot. This popular thinking is backed by the research: scholarly studies have piled up showing that race and gender diversity in school and the workplace can increase creative thinking and improve performance, whereas excessive homogeneity can lead to stagnation and poor problem-solving.[27]

Much of academia has itself stopped short in both the understanding and practice of true diversity—the diversity of ideas. We see this hostility to intellectual diversity and the competition of ideas in the sensational stories of violent campus mobs shutting down controversial speakers, for example. While these are isolated cases, I hear from students and faculty all the time with views outside the mainstream, who feel uncomfortable openly sharing what they actually think. As Greg Lukianoff and Jonathan Haidt chronicle in their 2018 bestseller *The Coddling of the American Mind*, many young Americans are learning that people they disagree with are not to be listened to respectfully and debated; they are to be silenced and driven out of the public square ("de-platformed" in modern academic parlance).

Recently, a team of scholars from six universities studying ideological diversity in the behavioral sciences published a paper in the journal *Behavioral and Brain Sciences* that details a shocking level of political groupthink in academia. For example, the authors show that for every politically conservative social psychologist in academia there are about fourteen liberal social psychologists.[28] That's not a problem on its face until you consider that in one survey cited, 82 percent of social psychologists admitted they would be less likely to support hiring a conservative colleague than a liberal scholar with equivalent qualifications.[29]

Unfair? Yes. But once again, the more dangerous effect of shutting down competition is on excellence. As the authors of the preceding study write, "Increased political diversity would improve social psychological science by reducing the impact of bias mechanisms such as confirmation bias, and by empowering dissenting minorities to improve the quality of the majority's thinking." One of the study's authors, Professor Philip E. Tetlock of the University of Pennsylvania, put it to me more bluntly. Expecting trustworthy results on politically charged topics from an "ideologically incestuous community," he explained, is "downright delusional."

The trend to shut down the competition of ideas on college and university campuses is harmful to research and instruction and is harmful to the unity of our country—because too many in the next generation of leaders are learning to despise and ostracize, rather than understand and engage, those with whom they disagree. This is not about right versus left. Discrimination against the political right today could be discrimination against the political left tomorrow, and it would be equally damaging.

If the competition of ideas is so great, does it mean we should agree on nothing? No. We do need to agree on some moral foundations in our arguments. If the Red Sox sought to end the game with a higher score, and the Yankees' objective was to end the game with the cleanest uniforms, the competition would not be meaningful or productive. Likewise, we need common societal objectives in the competition of ideas.

What are they? Let me offer a few for politics and policy today.

According to the American Founders, the moral core of the American experiment is that we are all trying to build a society that is fair, free, and abundant in opportunity for all people—especially those who would not enjoy these things anyplace else. The objective is that each of us, including the most vulnerable, can pursue the happiest life possible.

In his "Thoughts on Government," John Adams argued that "the happiness of society is the end of government," and, therefore, that the "form of government, which communicates ease, comfort, security, or in one word happiness to the greatest number of persons, and in the greatest degree, is the best."[30] To that end, as Adams's phrasing later enshrined in the Massachusetts Constitution put it, the government is "instituted for the common good; for the protection, safety, prosperity and happiness of the people; and not for the profit, honor or private interest of any one man, family, or class of men."[31]

We may disagree—we *should* disagree—over how best to achieve safety, prosperity, and happiness for the most people, and we should compete over the best way to help all people build better lives. To do so, however, we must maintain the shared objectives and moral core around which a true competition of ideas should radiate.

When the moral consensus to build a society that serves everyone collapses, then the means to reach that (former) consensus start to crash into each other head-on. They become the ends in themselves, untethered to moral principles, and the two sides start trying to win by any means necessary. When each side attacks the other as in a Holy War—when leaders question the motives of the other side rather than their ideas and pit Americans against each other—then the moral consensus has shattered and there is nothing around which a true competition of ideas can radiate.

Sound familiar? Maybe like today's political and policy debates, which are so bitter that we are willing to destroy people's lives and reputations for having the temerity to run for office or serve in government at a high level? The debasement of political and policy debates in the last few years reminds me of economic activity ungoverned by rules and basic morality—like a city where commerce is controlled by the Mob. Want to start a business? I hope you didn't like those kneecaps too much.

You may point out that there are some bad actors out there with stupid ideas. I agree. But the vast majority of Americans on both sides of the issues today are good and decent, and want to make the country better. And even if some ideas are beyond the pale, it is always worth confronting them with the best arguments, and without contempt—if our objective is to win over people who are undecided, and we care about the quality of our own character.

My opening question in this chapter—wouldn't life be better without competition?—was a red herring, or course. It is true that there are forces in American life pushing us toward the idea that competition is danger-ous and bad, but if you are like most Americans, and especially if you are still reading this book, you prob-ably don't think that.

The United States has led a philosophical revolu-tion in a lot of ways over the past two centuries. As I alluded to earlier, arguably the greatest of these is the popular recognition that competition brings out the best in us, if it is properly bounded and practiced by moral people. The World Values Survey (WVS) asks respondents to say which statement they agree with more: "Competition is good. It stimulates people to work hard and develop new ideas" or "Competition is harmful. It brings out the worst in people." The most recent survey found that Americans were nearly ten times as likely to say "Competition is good" as to say "Competition is harmful."[32]

There will always be people who see this attitude as evidence of "false consciousness," Marx's explanation for beliefs people hold that prevent them from appreciating their own social or economic exploitation. But such arguments are rare.

The United States' greatest contribution to world prosperity has been the cultural innovation of embracing competition in economics and politics. In my lifetime, democratic capitalism has made a world that was mostly poor into one that is mostly not. I am deeply proud to be part of a society that helped to lift up billions of people all around the world.

What I am *not* proud of is our increasing resistance to competing ideas, right here at home in our politics, in media, and on campuses. So how do we solve it? We need leaders who—while holding their own opinions—tolerate others', because they recognize that iron sharpens iron ideologically; that diversity in *all* forms is where our strength and unity are to be found.

Actually, that's still not good enough. As I said at the outset, tolerance and civility are too low a standard for a great country based on competitive excellence. You need to be *grateful* for the other side, just as you should be grateful for having more than one team in your favorite sports league and more than one brand of ice cream at the supermarket.

Sound crazy in the case of people who disagree with you? I don't think so. I've given hundreds of speeches in which I ask very partisan audiences: How many of you wish we lived in a one-party state? I always get zero hands (and I actually think zero hearts, too). What does that mean? If you don't want to live in a one-party state, then—like it or not—you just told me you are grateful for the other party.

That doesn't mean you agree with the other side. If you're a conservative, you disagree with people who you believe will increase taxes, increase regulations, make it harder to create jobs, and want to weaken our military. If you're a liberal, you disagree with people who will cut social spending, reduce taxes for the wealthy, and get us involved in foreign entanglements.

But don't turn disagreement into ingratitude. We live in a society in which people can disagree without fear of the government silencing dissent. We have decided together as Americans to set laws and social norms to make this possible, recognizing that we don't want to suppress the other side's ideas any more than we want them to suppress ours. We are grateful for *our* freedoms, and so we are grateful for *their* freedoms.

How can all this competition bring about greater national unity? While our preferred means to fully meet our national objective of equal opportunity are the focus of politics and activism, the objective itself—an ahistoric miracle—should be the subject of celebration across the spectrum of ideas. The Fourth of July should give us all a good feeling because of our underlying commitments to our fellow men and women, and the pride that comes from remembering our ancestors, who rose from nothing to earn their success in America. Unlike most places in the world, we compete to live up to our own ideals and make the country better for all. Enjoy the fact that we can compete by day, but then celebrate together when the fireworks begin.

There is a special pride that comes from fighting for the right of all sides to hold and express their ideas. We have disdain for the one-party dictatorships around the world; we make fun of fake elections in places like

Cuba. There is a special bond among Americans who stand up for one another when they disagree. Have you done that recently? If not, you're missing out on a great source of joy. If you're still not convinced, try the following and see how it makes you feel. Defend someone with whom you disagree, simply because he or she has a right to an opinion and the right to be heard. Take note that your heart will be on fire when you do it. That's because it's morally right, and your heart knows it.

Now go do it over and over.

Chapter 8
Please Disagree with Me

Both Robert "Robby" George and Cornel West are professors at Princeton University, globally renowned for their contributions to the field of political philosophy. That's where the similarities end.

George is one of the nation's most prominent conservative Christian intellectuals. A devout Catholic, he has written numerous books and articles opposing same-sex marriage and the "dogmas of liberal secularism." He drafted the Manhattan Declaration, a manifesto signed by dozens of Christian leaders who promised resistance against any effort to "compel our institutions to participate in abortions, embryo-destructive research, assisted suicide and euthanasia . . . [or] to force us to bless immoral sexual partnerships, treat them as marriages or the equivalent, or refrain from proclaiming the truth, as we know it, about morality and immorality and marriage and the family."[1] Perhaps unsurprisingly, he is also a Republican.

Cornel West is Robby George's ideological opposite—one of the nation's most prominent progressive thinkers. A professor of religion and African American studies, he is the honorary chairman of Democratic Socialists of America, a self-described anti-imperialist, and a sworn enemy of "the brutality of profit-driven capitalism." He was one of Barack Obama's harshest critics because, he says, Obama was "a black mascot of Wall Street oligarchs and a black puppet of corporate plutocrats."[2] West supported Bernie Sanders for the presidency in 2016. He is well known for the hip-hop and spoken-word albums he has released (he describes himself as a "jazz freedom fighter"), including *Sketches of My Culture* and *Street Knowledge*, which engage with the themes of his political work. He advocates civil disobedience and social activism.

What could be more combustible than a debate between George and West, who disagree vehemently on most issues, including human sexuality, race, identity, economics, and abortion? It has all the ingredients for pure vitriol. Want a brief taste of the terrible things they say about each other?

"I have a deep love for this brother. I have a deep

respect for this brother." That's Cornel West, referring to Robby George.[3]

"We're united to each other in love, in true fraternal affection," says George about West. "When I call Brother Cornel 'Brother Cornel' I mean he's my *brother*."

"We revel in each other's humanity," says West. "We share a fundamental commitment to the life of the mind and the world of ideas. We've had a chance to teach and lecture around the country, and so when I see him, I don't see him first and foremost as a conservative thinker, Catholic philosopher, one of the major political theorists of our day. I see him as my brother."

That's not what you were expecting. When contempt between partisans has become so common, what could possibly explain their personal warmth toward each other?

The most plausible explanation is that George and West have figured out a way to evade conflict. Perhaps they have found a few areas of common ground. Perhaps they have agreed to avoid disagreement, like those old British men's clubs that, for the sake of peace, prohibited discussions of politics and religion.

Maybe this is the answer to the culture of contempt. If we avoid the intellectually and morally fraught territory of politics and policy, we'll be able to live harmonious lives, even among our intellectual opponents.

Disagreements out of sight . . . contempt out of mind. That must be it.

To understand the relationship between friendship and disagreement, we need to go back in time a couple of millennia, to the philosophy of Aristotle.[4]

In his *Nicomachean Ethics,* Aristotle wrote that there were three kinds of friendship: The first and lowest form of friendship is that based on utility, wherein both people derive some benefit from each other. You have this kind of friendship with someone you know in business. Let's say Mike is one of your distributors, and he's your friend. He sells you bolts of fabric and you need them because you make shirts. While you probably never see each other outside work, you are nice to Mike, and Mike is nice to you. It's a transactional relationship in pecuniary terms. You need each other and are useful to each other.

You work hard not to disagree with Mike. If you like President Trump and Mike makes a derogatory remark about him, you smile and change the subject. Why? Because you don't want to mess up a perfectly good business relationship over something peripheral like politics.

The next level of friendship for Aristotle is based on pleasure; both people are drawn to the other's wit, intelligence, talent, good looks, or other attractive qualities. Say you have a friend named Mary. Every time you're around Mary, you learn something new. You love her mind. She's so interesting. Or maybe she's incredibly funny or has some other quality that makes her pleasant to be around.

As with Mike, you try to avoid disagreeing with Mary on something like politics. You know each other, but probably aren't close enough to risk a confrontation she might take personally. You don't want to stop enjoying her wonderful qualities because she is offended by your views.

Your friendship with Mary is slightly more virtuous than your friendship with Mike, because rather than needing something from her, you like her for the interior or exterior beauty that you want more of. It is a friendship, in essence, based on wanting to be near something that's good. It's still an imperfect friendship, however, because it is inward-facing. "Those who love for the sake of pleasure do so for the sake of what is pleasant to themselves," Aristotle writes. As a result, both of these forms of friendship are "incidental" and are "easily dissolved . . . if the one party is no longer pleasant or useful." If you quit the shirt-making business, you might never see Mike again, and you probably won't miss him much. If your interests change or her jokes get old, you and Mary will probably drift apart.

The highest form of friendship—the "perfect friendship" in Aristotle's telling—is one based on willing the good of the other and a shared sense of what is virtuous and true. Let's say you have an old friend named Frank. You love Frank, not because you do business with him (maybe you do, maybe you don't) or because he is funny and smart (he may or may not be), but because you share a deep moral concern for something outside yourselves. Maybe it's a love for God or a passion for a particular cause. Whatever it is, Aristotle would say you and Frank are "alike in virtue."

No doubt your friendship with Frank is useful and pleasurable—because good and virtuous people can also be useful and pleasant. Unlike friendships of utility and pleasure, however, which tend to dissipate, your friendship with Frank is lasting because it is based on something deeper: shared virtues and common ideals. You and Frank can probably expect to be friends for the rest of your lives.

What about disagreement? Unlike with Mike and Mary, with whom you avoid disagreement, with Frank you don't fear it. Your friendship is not fragile. You disagree on politics? Big deal. You want the other to see a better means to pursue your shared ends, and you naturally have different views on how to do that. You genuinely want to know *why* Frank thinks something you think is incorrect.

While you disagree, that doesn't mean you are disagreeable. When Frank asserts something you don't think is right, you don't tell him he is an idiot and should shut up. That would be contemptuous—an attempt to shut him down, which is exactly the opposite of what you want for and from Frank. Instead, you disagree, listen, and consider the merits of his arguments. Remember, the goal is not to show you are right and he is stupid; it is to achieve the shared objective.

You can use this framework to understand other kinds of relationships, even marriage. A marriage of utility is transactional—marrying someone for his or her money, for example. Obviously, this happens all the time, but no one thinks it's a good or stable "till death do you part" kind of setup, which is why people make jokes about it all the time. Alternatively, you can marry someone because you admire the person so much. But if that's as far as the relationship goes, the admiration will eventually fade and thus, usually, so will the love.

A lot of people see romantic love only through the lens of utility and pleasure. That is why so many assume that it will naturally fade and ultimately disappoint. This is the basic idea behind Emily Brontë's famous poem "Love and Friendship":

Love is like the wild rose-briar,
Friendship like the holly-tree—
The holly is dark when the rose-briar blooms
But which will bloom most constantly?

The wild rose-briar is sweet in spring,
Its summer blossoms scent the air;
Yet wait till winter comes again
And who will call the wild-briar fair?

Then scorn the silly rose-wreath now
And deck thee with the holly's sheen,
That when December blights thy brow
He still may leave thy garland green.[5]

It's a lovely poem, but Brontë's comparison between love and friendship is a false one. You don't have to choose, if you base your marriage on Aristotle's perfect friendship instead of utility or pleasure. You might want to have someone who will support you, and you may find the other person physically beautiful. But in the end, what holds you together for the rest of your life is a shared passion for the good of the other and what is right and true. That means a shared belief in the welfare of the kids, for example, and a shared commitment to your religious and philosophical beliefs.

One of the American Catholic Church's greatest communicators of the past century was Fulton Sheen, Bishop of Rochester, New York. Bishop Sheen had a popular television show and wrote bestselling books, such as the one my wife and I especially like: *Three to Get Married.* We use it in marriage-preparation classes we teach for engaged couples. In that book, Bishop Sheen teaches that the secret to a good marriage is a shared belief that God (the marriage's "third spouse") must be the most important thing in either person's life—not the husband or wife.[6]

Does that sound odd to you? It was hard for me and my wife to comprehend at first, too. While we are Catholics, it felt as though we were putting something in the middle of what should be sacrosanct. But that is the wrong way of seeing it. The objective is—even as we change over the course of our lives—to express our love for each other more deeply each year as a reflection of our shared love for God. This kind of marriage is a perfect friendship, under Aristotle's definition.

Does this mean the best marriage is all agreement? Absolutely not. My wife is Spanish, and there's a daily dose of passionate disagreement around my house. But while disagreement weakens the first two types of marriages, it strengthens the Aristotelian kind—as long as it focuses on shared ends and is pursued in the right sort of way. When we argue, it is almost inevitably over the best way to do things we agree about—bringing up our kids to be excellent people, for example.

I have obviously contradicted my opening claim in this chapter, that the secret to avoiding contempt is to avoid disagreement. And, in fact, Robby George and Cornel West contradict this as well. In West's words, "I see [Robby] as my friend and someone who has . . . a right to be wrong." As George notes in return, "We agree on almost nothing."

Just as Aristotle predicted, the deep friendship of Robby George and Cornel West is not predicated on finding areas of agreement or avoiding conflict. It requires disagreement, based on a shared quest for what is good and true and lifts up others, particularly those with less power and prestige than either of them possesses. As George explains, "The magic of our work together is exposing our students . . . to a situation where they really are hearing the competing arguments of two guys who are pretty passionate about their opinions, have pretty strong views, but are willing to argue with each other civilly, to engage each other's arguments, to listen, to be willing to learn from the other guy as well as to teach, and to have no thought about calling each other names or shouting at each other. I think the students in that circumstance learn not only by the content of what we say but just by the example of how we conduct ourselves. So, teaching with Cornel has been among the best experiences that I've had and I think that my students have had in my thirty-plus years at Princeton."

West and George don't put aside their differences and seek the mushy middle. They revel in their disagreements. "I have no particular love for armistices," George says. "What Professor West and I are about is conversations—getting at the truth, not just finding a way to agree, or a way to avoid difficult issues on which people disagree. But to have a conversation—a conversation whose aim is getting both of the interlocutors, or everybody concerned, a little nearer the truth."

Indeed, in 2017, they wrote a joint statement on the importance of truth seeking and freedom of thought and expression, which includes these words:

> None of us is infallible. Whether you are a person of
> the left, the right, or the center, there are reasonable

people of goodwill who do not share your fundamental convictions. . . . All of us should be willing—even eager—to engage with anyone who is prepared to do business in the currency of truth-seeking discourse by offering reasons, marshaling evidence, and making arguments. The more important the subject under discussion, the more willing we should be to listen and engage—especially if the person with whom we are in conversation will challenge our deeply held—even our most cherished and identity-forming—beliefs. . . .

Our willingness to listen to and respectfully engage those with whom we disagree (especially about matters of profound importance) contributes vitally to the maintenance of a milieu in which people feel free to speak their minds, consider unpopular positions, and explore lines of argument that may undercut established ways of thinking. Such an ethos protects us against dogmatism and groupthink, both of which are toxic to the health of academic communities and to the functioning of democracies.[7]

Here are two intellectuals who disagree as strenuously as any two people you can imagine. Yet they love each other. They respect each other. They call each other brother. Imagine if this were more common across academia. Imagine if it were more common across America. Imagine if you had it in your own life.

Is that possible?

Maybe you are detecting that there are similarities between the last chapter and this one. I actually conceived of them as one big chapter. Why? Because disagreement is just another way of saying "competition of ideas." The reason disagreement—properly undertaken— strengthens a perfect friendship is because competition makes things better. And disagreeing better, not less, is what we need to lessen contempt in America and bring our country back together.

Let's imagine for a moment that you and I are both passionate about alleviating poverty and helping more people achieve the American Dream. Those are really good, wholesome American values. But we disagree over how best to address the problem. One of us thinks that the best way to help the poor is with more government spending and a more generous social safety net. The other thinks the best way is through less government help, more incentives to work, and the power of free enterprise. We're in so much agreement about the underlying principle that we compete with each other on better ways to do it, and the result of that disagreement radiating around a common moral core will be better, more innovative public policies for the people we are trying to help. That's the essence of what Aristotle would call "political friendship." While perhaps not as intimate or noble as virtuous friendship, political friendship nevertheless is concerned with the common good and pursues shared ends.

Such political friendships are particularly suited to democracies, Aristotle wrote, because "in tyrannies, friendship and justice hardly exist, [while] in democracies they exist more fully; for where the citizens are equal they have much in common." To maintain Aristotelian political friendship in a democracy, however, we must maintain "unanimity" around that common moral core. "Such unanimity is found among good men; for they are unanimous both in themselves and with one another . . . they wish for what is just and what is advantageous, and these are the objects of their common endeavor as well."

When we lose sight of the shared just ends of our common endeavor, Aristotle writes, then friendship dissipates and "each man wishing for advantage to himself criticizes his neighbor and stands in his way." Eventually, "if people do not watch it carefully the common weal is soon destroyed. The result is that they are in a state of faction, putting compulsion on each other but unwilling themselves to do what is just." Those words, written in 350 BC, are a pretty apt description of the state of American politics today.

Virtuous Aristotelian friendship centered on loving our country and respectful disagreement is what we need in America. If you've got a better way to help poor people, I want to hear it. If I don't think it's a good enough way to help poor people, I'm going after your argument with everything I've got. You actually can't exercise the Aristotelian virtue adequately unless there's disagreement. The highest expression of this Aristotelian ideal is that two people totally disagree on a substantive thing but are willing to debate each other on it, precisely because they both care so much about the underlying issue on which they agree. That's when America is absolutely at its best.

All this is pretty theoretical, I realize. This is supposed to be a practical book, so you might be thinking, "OK, Brooks, give me some good rules on how to make this national healing happen, because all I see out there are insults, hatred, and vitriol." Here you go.

Rule 1. Find your Robby, Cornel, or Frank.

If you don't have any level-three Aristotelian friendships with people with different ideologies, you can't have the kind of productive disagreement that Robby and Cornel have. Each of us needs that kind of friendship so as to learn and practice the skill of disagreement in a spirit of love and warm-heartedness. You might be avoiding disagreements with the Mikes and Marys of your life, but if there aren't any Franks when it comes to big issues, especially politics and policy, you have a problem. Without Franks, you don't develop the ability to disagree constructively with others, so when there is political disagreement, it's fight or flight. Lacking practice, you get defensive and angry. That's failure, and when we scale it up to the national level, the results are what we see around us today.

If you don't have any Franks in your life, you need to ask *why not*. One reason is probably that we are less and less likely to meet reasonable people with good values and opposing ideas.

In times past, in most places it was hard to avoid Democrats if you were a Republican, and vice versa. In my own neighborhood in Seattle as a kid, there were families with Republican-voting parents and Democrat-voting parents. Mayors came from both parties, as did our representatives in Congress. I don't remember people getting completely freaked out when someone from the other party won. When I go back to Seattle today, it is totally different—a political monoculture. Republicans are so rare that the city has gone to mayoral elections between the top three vote-getters in the open primary, which means three Democrats, ranging from left to far left. As a result, it is hard to find people with real friends who disagree with them, and I have noticed that a lot of people are pretty bad at disagreement. In a public Seattle City Council meeting in 2017, a member of the council declared that she did not have a single Republican friend.[8] It should have appalled everyone there, but instead it was an applause line in what has become a one-party culture.

The same phenomenon holds in places all over America, on both the right and left. Congressional districts are increasingly uncompetitive between the parties, meaning that control of Congress comes down to just a handful of remaining swing districts. If you are in Seattle, conservatives are usually people you hear *about*, not *from*. Furthermore, what you hear about them is usually carefully curated by your favorite media outlet, which shares your dim view of people on the right. The same goes for liberals in rural Texas; you probably don't know many, or any, and hear about *them* on talk radio and conservative cable television.

If you are committed to better disagreement, you generally need a wider circle of friends, which is easier said than done. That means going places outside your traditional circles and making the effort to get to know people with different values in a deep way. This is hard, not just because you have to find them, but also because you have to listen. (Our society has become pretty incompetent when it comes to listening.) If you stay on Facebook reading angry articles about the other side, you'll never get there.

Does this seem obvious to you? It shouldn't. Lots of people believe they are deeply engaged in making their communities better by staying abreast of politics and policy, and getting involved in advocacy and activism. That's great, but it isn't enough. Doing these things today practically guarantees that you will be cloistered among those who already share all of your views. You need to accompany this with outreach efforts to people with *different* views. Go out and find them.

And then you need to engage them in a sincere, kind, respectful way. How? Read on.

Rule 2. Don't attack or insult. Don't even try to win.

What do you do once you have an honest disagreement with someone on the other side? Start by throwing away everything you've ever learned about winning.

Have you ever won an argument? According to Dale Carnegie, author of *How to Win Friends and Influ-*

ence People, which I referenced a few chapters ago, the answer is *no*. "You can't win an argument," Carnegie writes. "You can't because if you lose it, you lose it; and if you win it, you lose it. Why? Well, suppose you triumph over the other man and shoot his argument full of holes and prove that he is *non compos mentis*. Then what? You will feel fine. But what about him? You have made him feel inferior. You have hurt his pride. He will resent your triumph."[9]

Carnegie sums it up with this old verse:

A man convinced against his will
Is of the same opinion still.

The point of disagreement—if disagreement is to make us better and draw us together—is never winning. It certainly isn't to attack someone else. It is to enrich the discussion, test out your point of view in a respectful way, and persuade someone you care about.

We see destructive disagreement all the time when cable TV hosts bring on guests with opposing views, not to present viewers with different perspectives, but with the sole purpose of attacking them and "winning" an argument. Oftentimes the guest is some hapless person who wrote or said or did something absurd and can't really defend his position. The "debate" reminds me of the old Harlem Globetrotters traveling road show. They staged a game with fictional rivals called the Washington Generals, who got whipped and humiliated, night after night. Except the Generals were paid participants, whereas the TV show guests are unwitting victims. The point is that it's not meant to be a fair fight. The argument serves no purpose other than to allow the host to engage in posturing for the true believers on her own side. The host slings ad hominem attacks at the guest, makes him look ridiculous, and then thanks him for coming on— which is only intended as self-congratulation for having a "balanced" discussion. Later, the clip goes up on YouTube under the title "[Insert host name] DESTROYS [Insert guest name]."

We should never follow this model when we interact with people with whom we disagree. If we are going to engage in disagreement, we should do so in good faith. To do anything less is to short-circuit the competition of ideas.

There's a practical reason for engaging with respect, and there's a moral reason.

Here's the practical reason: almost no one is ever insulted into agreement. Recently, I saw a tweet from a conservative advocacy group dedicated to educating college students about economic responsibility and free-market principles. I'm sympathetic to those things, so I paused to look at it. It was addressed to progressives, and here's what it said:

> Dear liberal snowflakes: Nothing is free. Crying doesn't solve problems. Screaming doesn't make you right. Not everyone is a winner. There are no "Safe Spaces."

Can you imagine some liberal college student seeing that tweet and saying, "Nothing's free? I never realized it until just now. Crying doesn't solve problems? Wow. I wish somebody had told me that before." No, every liberal who saw that message thought one thing: *What jerks.*

It's not just conservatives who do this. Recently, during an event in India, Hillary Clinton made a claim about Trump supporters—in the form of a statement *to* them (even though they were not in attendance): "You know, you didn't like black people getting rights; you don't like women, you know, getting jobs; you don't want to, you know, see that Indian American succeeding more than you are."[10] That will win over approximately zero Trump supporters to Mrs. Clinton's point of view.

In fact, this approach is even worse than merely not persuading people. Research shows that insults actually intensify people's opposition to one's point of view. A classic 1967 study published in the *Journal of Experimental Social Psychology*, "Negative Persuasion via Personal Insult," demonstrated what we call the "boomerang effect," a phenomenon that occurs when you insult somebody and, in doing so, actually cause them to harden their views.[11] The researchers, from Yale University, showed that if people change their views at all, the odds are more than three-to-one that they will become more extreme in their original position.

We all can relate to this. Last year, I was at a fancy party, making small talk with people I didn't know very well. A woman asked my opinion on a common public policy issue. I gave it to her, in mild terms, in part because I suspected she disagreed and this was not the "safe space" of an Aristotelian virtuous friendship. She immediately flushed and said that I was "an obnoxious person." I was taken aback because that's a weirdly aggressive response. But even stranger, I suddenly felt my opinion on that issue become very strong. Boomerang!

There are two possible explanations for this boomerang effect. One is the "social equity mechanism." When a person exposes his views to challenge, it represents a "social investment" and he expects some level of "social reward" in the form of acceptance or approval. If that expectation is violated with insults, he responds by adopting an even more extreme oppositional position.

Imagine that a supporter of Second Amendment rights asks a supporter of gun control what informs his beliefs. If, rather than acknowledge the gun-rights supporter's openness to hearing a different side, the gun-control advocate says, "Well, if you're against gun control, you clearly don't care about the lives of children," then it's not hard to see why the individual might take an even stronger stance on gun rights after that conversation. As the Yale researchers noted, "It is as though the victim says, 'I'll show you. If you're going to insult me when I give you the chance to change my opinions, I not only won't change them, I'll make them more objectionable to you.'"

The second explanation for the boomerang effect is called the "imagined supporter mechanism," by which the insulter leaves the impression that all people arguing his particular side of the issue are as unpleasant as he is. The supporter of gun rights, knowing few gun-control advocates, might conclude that all advocates of gun control are rude and insulting, like this person. The researchers note, "It is as if the victim says, 'Well, if a lout like you has those opinions, they can't be right.'" Our perceptions may not fully reflect reality, but in both cases, the victim digs in and becomes less likely to listen to opposing points of view.

This is especially likely to happen when people are so siloed ideologically. When I go onto a college campus and say something favorable about free enterprise, it is quite possible that students have never heard someone making this argument. If this is true, then they will form their opinion about people with my point of view almost entirely from their perceptions about me. One bit of sarcasm, one little insult, and there's the boomerang. This is a big responsibility, as I often explain to young people who share my views. Among other things, I strongly urge them not to bring controversialists—those who simply seek to stir up ill will and protest—to campus, because via the boomerang effect, it will make the problems of campus monoculture worse, not better.

We know that insults are mostly ineffective and can make our interlocutors even more opposed to our point of view. These are practical reasons to avoid them, but there's the moral reason, too: they're just plain wrong. We simply should not put up with insults, whether from the other side or our own. Indeed, I'll take it a step further. When someone on *your* side insults people on the *other* side, it is your responsibility to take it personally and stand up for those with whom you disagree.

Here's a question I often ask audiences when I'm giving a speech: "How many of you love somebody with whom you disagree politically?" Almost every hand goes up, every time. Whether you are liberal, conservative, or in between, I'll bet you would raise your hand, too.

That means that when someone who agrees with you insults people on the other side, they are insulting your loved ones. You should be offended, and you should take the moral challenge. Someone on your side is insulting your sister. How do you feel about that? I realize you disagree with your sister, but it's not alright for some guy you just met to say that she's stupid or evil. What should you do? Simple: stick up for her. If you don't defend her from slander, you have become complicit in it.

When we hear insults, we need to push back. We can't wait for politicians on the national stage to exhibit better behavior; we need to demand it at the grassroots level. We need to defend people with whom we disagree when they're insulted by people with whom we do agree. No matter what, we need to police our own behavior so that we don't fall into the trap of insulting the other side. That's the mark of good character and moral leadership—and an important step on the path to defeating the culture of contempt.

Rule 3. Never assume the motives of another person.

The 2016 presidential debates between Donald Trump and Hillary Clinton got the highest television ratings in the history of televised debates. For example, 71.6 million Americans tuned in on October 19, 2016.[12] Were they eager to see reasoned arguments, respectful disagreement, and thought-out policy positions? Of course not. The day of that debate, the watercooler conversations were about what zinger Clinton would use to shut down Trump and what outrageous insult Trump would launch back. The day after, the video clip flying around social media was this exchange:

Trump: Putin . . . from everything I see, has no respect for this person.

Clinton: Well, that's because he'd rather have a puppet as president of the United States.

Trump: No puppet! No puppet!

Clinton: And it's pretty clear . . .

Trump: You're the puppet!

Clinton: It's pretty clear you won't admit . . .

Trump: No, you're the puppet!

OK, I admit I cried with laughter as I watched this. My teenage kids did, too, and to this day, they call each other "Puppet."

Perhaps this is good entertainment, but it improves the debate in no way, shape, or form. Why? Because it is an example of the *argumentum ad hominem*, a fallacious debate strategy in which the background or perceived motives of one's interlocutor are attacked to invalidate his or her argument. "You can't trust anything the other person says on Russia, because he/she is secretly soft on Russia!" This kind of debate disregards the objective merits of arguments. Instead, it stands up and then knocks down bad-faith arguments—the supposedly nefarious motives behind a given position, not the position itself.

Predictably, given the rhetoric of our leaders in America today, we increasingly engage in this kind of practice. Even on college campuses—with exceptions such as that of Cornel West and Robby George—where free speech and open debate are supposed to be inviolable, people are shouted down because of ideologies and values that are not even under debate, or because they have no standing due to their race or economic background.

This is intellectually weak. Imagine if Robby George accused Cornel West of holding his views because deep down he hates white people. It would foreclose their entire conversation. Yet that is more or less what we see every day today on campuses, on television, in politics, and on social media. To be sure, some people do harbor bad motives. And everybody knows about the horrific discrimination that stained our nation's past. But it is not reasonable to argue that malevolence or hatred are the animating forces behind the beliefs of the vast majority of Americans today.

Worse than being just unfair, such a belief is too often based in rank ignorance. How many times have you heard a conservative pundit say that Democrats want to keep poor people dependent on the government to keep them voting Democratic? Or a liberal pundit say that Republican tax policies are all about helping Republicans' wealthy friends?

The truth is that highly partisan conservatives and liberals are shockingly clueless about the other side—about their motives and everything else. One 2018 study from the *Journal of Politics* has revealed that the average Democrat believes that more than 40 percent of Republicans earn over $250,000 per year, when in fact just 2.2 percent do.[13] And Republicans believe that nearly 40 percent of Democrats are gay or lesbian, when just over 6 percent are.

In a related 2018 Pew survey, sizable majorities of rural, suburban, and urban residents said they understood the problems faced by Americans living in communities different from their own either very well or somewhat well.[14] Tellingly, however, equally significant majorities of rural, suburban, and urban residents expressed a belief that Americans who live in communities different from their own *don't* understand the problems *they* face. As this discrepancy indicates, we don't even know the extent to which we don't know our fellow citizens who are different from us. It's no coincidence that 63 percent of urban residents and 56 percent of rural residents believe that Americans who live in different types of communities than their own view them negatively.

If we don't even know the basic facts about the other side and can't relate to people living in different communities, why would we know anything about one another's motives?

Ad hominem arguments are a lazy expression of ignorance and should be avoided. If we can begin to take the arguments of our fellow citizens at face value, two things will improve: our ability to disagree productively and the policy outcomes at which we ultimately arrive.

Rule 4. Use your values as a gift, not as a weapon.

Ask yourself this question before you engage in disagreement: Am I using my values as a gift or as a weapon?

Values are supposed to be positive. Even if people disagree with them, they aren't supposed to harm others. We can't beat someone over the head with charity, for example. If we do, it's no longer charity. It's impossible to maintain the moral content of our values and use them as a weapon at the same time.

For example, let's say you are a pro-lifer on the abortion issue. If you go to people who are pro-choice and call them baby-killers, you're weaponizing your values and thus neutralizing their moral content. Perhaps you are pro-life because you believe life is a gift from God and think it's morally wrong to throw it away. However, if you call someone who disagrees with you a baby-killer, you haven't told the person who disagrees with you that life is a beautiful thing; you've called your opponent a murderer. You've hardened that person's opposition and neutralized the moral content of your own argument. Plus, you are almost certainly going to stimulate the boomerang effect, making that person even more vociferously pro-choice.

Two of the greatest moral values many of us share

as Americans are patriotism and faith. During a 2018 congressional special election in Pennsylvania, the Republican candidate declared that liberals hate America and hate God. "I've talked to so many of these on the left," he said. "I tell you, many of them have a hatred for our country. . . . I'll tell you some more—my wife and I saw it again today, they have a hatred for God."[15]

Loving America and loving God are both very positive things, in my view. Probably you agree, regardless of your politics. To use those positive values as a weapon and say that the other side hates America and hates God is deeply offensive and highly counterproductive. It alienates not only the liberals who were attacked, but also independents and conservatives who have loved ones who disagree with them on politics but know that they love America and God. This is a classic weaponization of values. It's not something that good or moral leaders should ever do.

We also see this in the gun debate. I didn't just make up the example I used earlier in this chapter. After the high school shooting in Parkland, Florida, I heard a cable news commentator say that NRA supporters care more about guns than children. The truth is that both sides of the gun debate want fundamentally good American things. One side wants to protect what they see as a fundamental freedom and their right to self-defense.

The other side is seeking the most effective way to protect children—and they believe that gun control is effective. Neither side is morally bankrupt; they just disagree. When either side uses those values to attack the other side, they neutralize the moral content of their argument and alienate potential allies.

The next time you are about to engage in disagreement over a contentious issue, ask yourself a question: Am I about to use my values as a gift, or as a weapon to attack the other side? If you are about to use them as a weapon, stop. Find a way to use your values as a gift instead.

Of course, there may be times when the goal is not to persuade but to energize true believers. For example, when a politician who wants the Republican nomination for president is standing up in front of a group of conservative activists, it's perfectly plausible that persuading liberals or independents is not his proximate goal at all. He wants to fire up his base so they will leave that hall and knock on doors, make phone calls, and turn out the vote for him.

There's nothing wrong with that. There's a place for energizing your base in politics. But there is a right way to energize your base and a wrong way.

It used to be that in American politics, most politicians worked to both fire up their core supporters *and* persuade those who were on the fence. They knew that they needed an energized base but also that turning out their base was not enough to win elections. Thus, as they rallied their core supporters they would at the same time try to reach out and work to persuade enough undecided voters to put them over the top on Election Day. The imperative to persuade the persuadables served as a check on how they energized their core supporters—because while they wanted to get their side excited to vote, they also did not want to say things that might alienate the undecideds whose votes they needed as well.

Today, it seems, persuasion is out the window. Elections have become base mobilization exercises, with both Republicans and Democrats competing to see who can energize their base more by throwing red meat into the crowd and insulting the other side. Whichever side is more worked up and angry on Election Day wins—or so the conventional wisdom has it.

This is an inherently unstable model for our democracy. Instead of swinging, the political pendulum careens violently back and forth as each side seeks to out-outrage the other. As a result, between elections, nothing gets done because both sides have such contempt for each other. The losing side seeks to stop any progress until they can win back power in the next election. Then the other side does the same. And on it goes.

It has gotten so bad that many good politicians increasingly believe they have no choice but to insult the other side or get out of politics. Among my friends in Congress, I hear it all the time. Here's the lament: People turn out for my campaign rallies to hear me trash the other side. If I don't do it, they will boo me, and my local talk radio host will say I'm weak!

My answer is always the same: Do what you know is right. How? Criticize those you disagree with without insulting them, questioning their motives, or weaponizing your values. There is a huge difference between saying "Candidate A's policies will decimate our military and put Americans at greater risk of a terrorist attack" and saying "Candidate A is cutting military spending because he wants ISIS to win."

In many cases, you can use the very same words and phrases as either a gift or a weapon. Take, for example, the phrase "Make America great again." Here is the first time the phrase was used in a presidential campaign:

I want more than anything I've ever wanted, to have an administration that will, through its actions, at home and in the international arena, let millions of people know that Miss Liberty still Lifts her lamp beside the golden door. . . . Let us send, loud and clear, the message that this generation of Americans intends to keep that lamp shining; that this dream, this last best hope of man on earth, this nation under God, shall not perish from the earth. We will instead carry on the building of an American economy that once again holds forth real opportunity for all, we shall continue to be a symbol of freedom and guardian of the eternal values that so inspired those who came to this port of entry. Let us pledge to each other, with this Great Lady looking on, that we can, and so help us God, we will make America great again.[16]

Don't remember this from the 2016 campaign? That's because those words were uttered by Ronald Reagan on September 1, 1980, during a speech delivered before the Statue of Liberty. Reagan coined the phrase "Make America great again." He used it as a gift, not a weapon.

Reagan did not hold back in his criticism of Jimmy Carter's record or his ideas. Reagan was tough. He explained what was at stake in the 1980 election. He laid blame for the results of failed policies at Jimmy Carter's feet. But never once did he say that Jimmy Carter hated America, was a crook, or wanted to see the American dream die. He knew Jimmy Carter was a good man who loved his country—he just had, in Reagan's opinion, the wrong ideas for how to make America great again.

Reagan used his values as a gift, not a weapon. He energized his base while simultaneously winning over a lot of persuadable Americans.

That is what America desperately needs today. As Robby George and Cornel West put it in their joint statement: "The maintenance of a free and democratic society require[s] the cultivation and practice of the virtues of intellectual humility, openness of mind, and, above all, love of truth. . . . Even if one happens to be right about this or that disputed matter, seriously and respectfully engaging people who disagree will deepen one's understanding of the truth and sharpen one's ability to defend it. . . . All of us should seek respectfully to engage with people who challenge our views."

If we follow these simple rules, we have no need to avoid disagreements. On the contrary, we can disagree fiercely without the unproductive, deeply unpleasant Holy War that is our politics today. We can respect others enough to give our views without saying that theirs are trash.

And there's a bonus. When I described the friendship between Robby and Cornel, were you maybe a tiny bit jealous? If so, that's because their friendship is a beautiful thing and a source of happiness for both men. You know how it feels when you make peace without compromising your principles. It just feels right.

We all need a friendship like that—a friendship that builds us up by challenging us to become wiser, kinder, and more thoughtful people. So find your Robby, your Cornel, or your Frank. Embrace better, not less, disagreement. Don't assume people's motives, never attack or insult anyone, and remember to share your values as a gift, not a weapon. Because in addition to improving our nation, following these rules of disagreement will give you a fighting chance to one day call someone you disagree with Brother or Sister.

It will give you the joy that comes only from perfect friendship.

Conclusion
Five Rules to Subvert the Culture of Contempt

Every parent knows by heart his or her kid's favorite book. You have to read it to them every single night, sometimes multiple times, for months and years on end. It's like something they'd make you do at Guantánamo, and it gets seared permanently into your brain. My poor dad could recite Dr. Seuss's *Yertle the Turtle*, word for word, until the day he died.

For whatever reason, my own kids loved *The Important Book* by Margaret Wise Brown, written in 1949. It goes through everyday things a child would see and lists what is "important" about them.

Here's one little snippet to give you an idea:

The important thing about rain is
that it is wet.

It falls out of the sky,
and it sounds like rain,
and makes things shiny,
and it does not taste like anything,
and is the color of air.
But the important thing about rain
is that it is wet.[1]

I always suspected that Margaret Wise Brown was secretly moonlighting as a beat poet. She would play the bongos for a minute, and then, while taking a deep drag on her cigarette, say, "The important thing about rain is that it is wet. *Can you dig it?*"

Anyway, I remember that book every time I'm finishing a new book of my own and am writing the conclusions chapter, which is supposed to sum up the important point of my book in a memorable way. So here goes, in the style of Margaret Wise Brown:

The important thing about contempt is
that it is bad for us.
Sometimes we don't like people who disagree
    with us,
and we want to tell them they are idiots,
and social media makes it easy to do,
and pundits get rich by doing it,

and maybe it seems that some of them deserve our
contempt.
But the important thing about contempt
is that it is bad for us.

(Cue the bongos.)

What is the cure for our culture of contempt? As I
have argued throughout, it's not civility or tolerance,
which are garbage standards. It is *love* for one another
and our country. Love is the "why" of the leaders that
can bring America back together, and of all of us in our
families and communities.

You might note that the title of this book is actually
a bit misleading. The problem I address is that we are
constantly hearing that those who disagree with us are
our enemies, and many Americans have begun to believe this. But in reality, these aren't my enemies at all;
rather, they are simply people with whom I disagree.

I am asking you to join me in a countercultural
movement. I don't know yet if it will be successful or
popular. If this were a book called *Liberals Are Evil*
or *Conservatives Are Stupid*, it would be a guaranteed
mega-bestseller and the call to action in the last chapter
would be simply to go along with what everybody else
is doing. Watch a ton of cable TV and read your favorite partisan columnists; silo your news feeds on social

media; curate your friends and stop talking to people on the other side; compare people you disagree with to Hitler or Stalin; make huge assumptions about others' motives; hate; hate; hate.

The call to action here is harder, because I'm asking you to join me and work to subvert the prevailing culture of contempt as a radical for love and decency. But I need to lay out the plan as specifically as possible, because it runs so counter to the currents of our prevailing culture.

So, culled from the lessons throughout this book, here are five simple rules to remember if you believe we can renew our nation and you want to be part of that movement.

Rule 1. Stand up to the Man. Refuse to be used by the powerful.

Most people don't believe they are being used by others. Why not? Think for a second about a manipulative leader—someone you know of who really uses people's hatred for his or her own goals of money, power, or fame. Got the image in your head?

Well, guess what? You have the wrong image, because that's someone you dislike. You are thinking of someone who might use others, but who can't use you, because you already see through him or her. The right image of a powerful manipulator is someone on *your side of the debate.* Maybe it's a media figure who always affirms your views, or a politician who always says what you think, or a professor who never challenges your biases. They say the other side is terrible, irredeemable, unintelligent, deviant, or anything else that expresses contempt—and say you should think these things as well.

As satisfying as it can feel to hear these things, remember: these people do not serve your interests. If you have gotten this far in this book, you (like me) have strong views on various subjects but hate the way we are being torn apart, which is what these powerful people are doing. Why do they do that? Because when they get you fired up, they make money, win elections, or get more famous and powerful.

To begin with, then, make an inventory of these kinds of figures in your life. Take your time; be honest. This is just for yourself; you don't have to post it on social media. Then set your strategy for rebellion.

Rebellion comes in one of two forms. The first is passive: tuning these manipulators out. This is most appropriate for those with whom you don't have any direct contact—a columnist or TV host, for example. Stop watching the show or reading the column. Ask yourself: Will I miss something I don't already think or know, or am I just scratching an itch? Remember: Unless the person is actually teaching you something or expanding your worldview and moral outlook, you are being used.

The second form is active—and harder: Stand up to people on your own side who trash people on the other side. It's never easy to stand up to our own friends, but contempt is destructive no matter who expresses it. You don't have to be a jerk about it. Simply be the person who gently defends those who aren't represented, even if you disagree with them. Will you get invited to fewer parties, have fewer followers on social media, and hear less gossip? Probably. But you know it's the right thing to do. And you will feel *great*.

Rule 2. Escape the bubble. Go where you're not invited, and say things people don't expect.

Just as a fire requires oxygen, the culture of contempt is sustained by polarization and separation. It is easy to express contempt for those with whom we disagree when we view them as "them" or never see them at all. Contempt is frankly much harder to express when we see one another as fellow human beings, as "us."

A simple way to start is by going to unfamiliar ideological territory. If you're a conservative, listen to National Public Radio in the morning a couple of days a week instead of watching *FOX & Friends*, or include a few pieces from the *Atlantic* in your list of articles to read. If you're liberal, from time to time put down the *Washington Post* (unless you're reading my columns) and read the *Wall Street Journal* editorial page, or add a few conservative podcasts to your rotation of offerings from more progressive hosts.

A more serious approach involves your portfolio of relationships. Ask yourself: Do I go places where my ideas are in the minority? Do I hear diverse viewpoints? Do I have personal friendships with people who do not share my politics? Answer honestly, and make an ideologically wider social circle this year's project.

Seeking out what those on the other side have to say will help you understand others better. You will be a stronger person, less likely to be aggrieved or feel unsafe when you hear alternative points of view. Plus, such understanding will also improve your ability to articulate and defend your own beliefs in a way that others find compelling, or least defensible. You might change a mind or two. And if your argument is weak, you'll be the first to know.

Escaping the bubble also means (to mix metaphors a little) breaking out of the shackles of identity. In America today, people primarily identify themselves in strong demographic terms, including political categories. To be sure, this identification can create a sense of belonging and power in numbers. But mostly it emphasizes our differences. That is ultimately a self-defeating proposition if what we want is a unified country that can cope with our shared challenges in the years ahead. It is a reduction to demographic identities that makes us distant and unrelatable to others and makes others seem foreign and contemptible to us.

By now readers know that one of my great moral heroes is the Dalai Lama, and I believe he understands the balance between common story and individual identity better than anyone I have ever met. Here are his words: "I'm Tibetan, I'm Buddhist, and I'm the Dalai Lama, but if I emphasize these differences, it sets me apart and raises barriers with other people. What we need to do is to pay more attention to the ways in which we are the same as other people."[2]

We are called to find common ground where it genuinely exists, improve our own arguments, and win over persuadable Americans by answering hostility with magnanimity, understanding, good humor, and love. We cannot do that while hiding in our narrow ideological foxholes. This is especially true for leaders, which every person reading this book is, or can be if you so choose.

Rule 3. Say no to contempt. Treat others with love and respect, even when it's difficult.

Contempt is the problem in our culture today, and it is never the solution. We are polarized and unable to make progress because contempt has created a bitter tribalism in America. Do not be part of this problem. No insults, no mockery. And as psychologist John Gottman taught us way back in chapter 1, no eye-rolling!

I must come back to a point I have made repeatedly: never treat others with contempt, *even if you believe they deserve it*. First, your contempt makes any persuasion of others impossible, because no one has ever been insulted into agreement. Second, you may be wrong to assume that certain people are beyond reason. I have given plenty of examples in this book of people forming unlikely bonds precisely because they didn't treat each other with contempt. Finally, contempt is always harmful for the contemptor. While it might feel good in the moment, it is the fast road to unhappiness and even poor health.

"How can I avoid contempt for someone who is immoral?" I hear that question every day. In virtually every case, those whom you consider to be immoral are not so in ways you care about, like compassion and fairness. They have different moral taste buds on issues like loyalty, purity, and authority, but that's all right. Focus on the things that are most important to both of you.

What about when *you* are the one treated with contempt? It won't be long before you are, if you are on social media or a campus or live in our society. What should be your reaction? The answer is to see it not as a threat but an opportunity. Why? Because another's expression of contempt toward you is your opportunity to change at least one heart—your own. Respond with warm-heartedness and good humor. Your life will change a little. You are *guaranteed* to be happier. Others might see it, and if it affects them at all, it will be to the good.

It sounds like I am telling you to be a nice person. That is correct. Being contemptuous and being nice are totally incompatible. Lest you worry that being nice is deleterious to your success in work and life—that you might look like a patsy—this book gave you a trainload of empirical evidence to the contrary. Jerks can do alright for a while, but in the end, nice guys (and girls) usually finish first.

For leaders who truly desire the common good—as opposed to manipulate the public for personal gain—repudiating contempt and embracing love for others means adopting an authoritative leadership model. Coercion, division, and polarization are ultimately counterproductive and never to be used. Rather, the goal should be to work to inspire others with a vision of hope and a model of inclusiveness toward others' ideas.

One last word on this topic. You might be feeling a little guilty right now. If you have been connected at all to political discussion over the last few years, you may have become a combatant in the war, and guilty of saying contemptuous things about, or to, others. I have, too. What do we do about that?

Remember a few chapters ago, when I compared our contempt addiction to alcoholism? For contempt addicts who are committed to change, there's a lesson for us from Alcoholics Anonymous. AA takes its members through twelve steps to recovery; step nine is: "Make direct amends to such people wherever possible, except when to do so would injure them or others."

Have you hurt someone with your harsh words, mockery, or dismissiveness? Are you among the millions of Americans who have abandoned a close relationship because of politics? It's time to apologize. Perhaps say, "I know we don't agree, but you are more important to me than our disagreement. Sorry I let our disagreement mess up our relationship." If the person won't accept your apology, that's a pity, but it still will help *your* heart.

Does this idea make you nervous? Maybe you'll need a couple of drinks first. (Just kidding.)

Rule 4. Disagree better. Be part of a healthy competition of ideas.

If you did nothing more than glance at the cover of this book, you might be tempted to conclude that my argument is to avoid being disagreeable by disagreeing less with others. By now you know that nothing could be further from my point.

Disagreement is good because competition is good. Competition lies behind democracy in politics, and markets in the economy. Markets and democracy are the two things that have made the United States into the most successful country in history, attracting the world's strivers, giving most readers of this book a good life, and creating a model for people all over the world. In politics and economics, competition—bounded by rule of law and morality—brings excellence.

As it is in politics and economics, so it is in the world of ideas. What is a competition of ideas called? "Disagreement." Disagreement helps us innovate, improve, correct, and find the truth.

Of course, the competition of ideas—like free markets and free elections—requires proper behavior to function.

No one thinks that hacking a voting machine is part of a healthy democracy, nor that cronyism and corruption are part of the way free enterprise is supposed to work. In fact, those things are the opposite of competition; they are ways to *avoid* competition. Likewise, anything that makes open, respectful disagreement difficult or impossible is incompatible with a true competition of ideas.

The most obvious way we shut down the competition of ideas today is by shutting out certain voices and viewpoints. Institutions can do this—think of the movement at some universities to "de-platform" objectionable people and views—but so can individuals when they curate their news and information in a way that excludes ideas with which they disagree.

Less obvious but even more important for the competition of ideas is our attitude toward others when we disagree with them. We are in our current mess of tribalism and identity politics not because of de-platforming or social media siloing—those are symptoms of the real problem, which is our attitude of contempt toward others. Contempt shuts down the competition of ideas.

The single biggest way a subversive can change America is not by disagreeing *less*, but by disagreeing *better*—engaging in earnest debate while still treating everyone with love and respect.

Rule 5. Tune out: Disconnect more from the unproductive debates.

The last four rules summed up the lessons in this book. However, I realize I have one more I need to give you before we finish. My guess is that you, like me, are superconnected to the world of ideas. That's great, but it can also be problematic.

For most of my life, I believed that to have a positive impact on the world, I needed to be as informed about it as possible. In my twenties, when I was making my living as a French horn player in Barcelona, and with no plans to change career and no interest in public policy, I nevertheless decided to subscribe to the *Economist* magazine. I simply felt that I needed more information about the world to be a better citizen.

Many people subscribe to this theory. The media industry certainly wants you to. But is it right? These days, is more information better than less for your ability to be a constructive and happy citizen? Making you a constructive and happy citizen certainly isn't the objective of much of the media today. Click on the app for your favorite newspaper and you will be immediately enmeshed in a complicated algorithm feeding you stories curated by your tastes and tendencies and specifically designed to keep you reading as long as possible. Social media sites are engineered to feed your addiction to dopamine, the neurotransmitter implicated in all addictive activities and substances.

The free flow of information is obviously important for a free society. Public ignorance is a threat to freedom, as it aids powerful individuals with the wrong motives. And I recommend full participation in the competition of ideas. But the importance of being an informed participant does not lead in any way to the conclusion that more media in your life is always and everywhere better for you, or for America. I hope I have convinced you in this book that social media is creating tremendous problems, as is the constant outrage on ideologically siloed cable television.

The solution is selectivity and rationing. Obliterate your silos by listening, reading, and watching media on the "other side." Get rid of your curated social media feeds. Unfollow public figures who foment contempt, even if you agree with them. Even better, cut way back on your social media use, perhaps limiting it to a few minutes a day. In addition to helping the country, you will be happier. A friend of mine—a well-known journalist with a large social media following—once confided in me that there is little that brings him more anxiety than checking his Twitter feed. As he clicks on his notifications, he can feel his chest tighten. Maybe you can relate to this. If so, take control.

Want to get really radical? Stop talking and thinking about politics entirely for a little while. Do a politics cleanse. For two weeks—maybe over your next vacation—resolve not to read, watch, or listen to anything about politics. Don't discuss politics with anyone. When you find yourself thinking about politics, distract yourself with something else. This is hard to do, of course, but not impossible. You just have to plan ahead and stand firm.

In discussing this proposal with friends and colleagues, I detect an inchoate fear. It goes something like this: "If I tune out politics, I may be happier, but it's irresponsible. The fascists"—my conservative friends here say "communists"—"will run across the country with abandon." This is a version of John Stuart Mill's maxim, "Bad men need nothing more to compass their ends than that good men should look on and do nothing."

Is that how you feel? Here's the truth: If you stop talking about politics for a couple of weeks, *nothing will change*, except you might get invited to more parties because you don't always talk about politics.

Besides, whether you know it or not, you probably need a break. Afterward, with a bit more perspective, you can come back to current events. Three predictions: First, you'll find that politics is a little like a daytime soap opera, of which you can skip a couple of weeks without losing track of the plot. Second, you'll see the outrage industrial complex in media and politics more clearly for what it is: a bunch of powerful people who want to keep you wound up for their own profit. Third, like any reformed addict, you'll see how much time you were wasting and how much you were neglecting people and things you truly love.

After you come back from your politics cleanse, how can you keep from falling back into your old patterns? Resolve to pay attention to *ideas*, not just politics. As I said at the very outset of this book, they aren't the same thing; ideas are like the climate, whereas politics is like the weather. The world is full of amateur political weather forecasters. The world needs more people who are thoughtful about the climate of ideas. Perhaps most important, while politics creates animus and contempt, people can generally disagree about ideas without bitterness. I know of no one who has stopped talking to a family member over disagreements about the merits of the idea of a universal basic income, for example.

I just reduced this whole book to a few lessons. Want it even simpler? Go find someone with whom you disagree; listen thoughtfully; and treat him or her with respect and love. The rest will flow naturally from there.

Think of it like missionary work. Missionaries are generally ordinary people with a vision for a better world that they want to share. They face a lot of opposition. In places like China, they are in physical danger, and even here in the United States, most people hear the knock on the door from missionaries and whisper, "Pretend we're not home!" But some open the door, and then some of those people listen and say, "I do want that." That's how proselytizing is supposed to work. Missionaries supply others with a new, clear, and purpose-filled vision, delivered with love and kindness (never contempt, if they want to succeed), and then give them the tools to make that vision a reality. And no matter how others receive their witness, they themselves wind up brimming with joy.

Near my home there is a Catholic retreat house where my wife and I teach marriage-preparation classes for engaged couples. (When we were engaged, we barely spoke a word of the same language. We don't recommend this for communication.) In the chapel, there is a sign posted over the door—not the door coming in, but rather the one going out into the parking lot. It is written for people to look at as they're leaving. It says, YOU ARE NOW ENTERING MISSION TERRITORY. The message is simple yet profound: you are here because you have found what is good and true, but you're going to go out where people haven't yet found what you've discovered. You have the privilege of sharing it, with joy, confidence, and love.

That shouldn't be just a religious message. It should be a message to all of us who want to make America and the world better. You *know* what our world needs: more love, less contempt. I hope that after reading this book, you have clear ideas on how you can be part of the movement to make it so and are fired up about the prospect. So as you put down this book, I have just one thing I want you to remember:

You are now entering mission territory.

Acknowledgments

My gratitude starts with two people: my colleague Marc Thiessen, a great writer and thinker who worked for many hours to shape a pile of notes and videos into what would become this book; and my research assistant Nathan Thompson, who made sure I was correct, consistent, comprehensible, and compassionate throughout, and who now heads off to start his doctorate and what will be a brilliant career as a scholar. Any errors in this book are mine alone, but the book itself would not exist without Marc and Nathan.

As this book is published, I am near the end of my decade-long tenure as president of the American Enterprise Institute. It has been the honor of my life to serve AEI and a privilege to be surrounded by colleagues who are intellectual warriors for human dignity and potential. Particular appreciation for help with *Love Your Enemies* goes to Jason Bertsch, John Cusey, Nick Eberstadt, David Gerson, Rachel Manfredi, Spencer Moore, and Charles Murray. And special thanks to Ceci Gallogly and Abby Guidera, who manage my office and my creative work—and thus, a big percentage of my life.

I am indebted to AEI's co-chairmen, Tully Friedman and Daniel D'Aniello, for their friendship and unfailing support, as well as to Ravenel Curry and his late wife, Beth, for their commitment to my work over the last decade. I am also grateful to AEI's Board of Trustees and National Council for their wisdom and guidance.

For support of AEI's Human Dignity Project, of which this book formed a part, I would like to thank the Dick and Betsy DeVos Foundation, the Doug and Maria DeVos Foundation, the Grover Hermann Foundation, the Kern Family Foundation, the Anschutz Foundation, Preston Butcher, Gary and Nancy Chartrand, Arthur A. Ciocca, Joseph W. Craft III and the Honorable Kelly Craft, Mike Fernandez, Ed and Helen Hintz, Jim Mooney, George and Linnea Roberts, and Steve and Amy Van Andel.

For their skill and guidance, I'm indebted to Eric Nelson, my editor at Broadside Books, and Lisa Adams, my literary agent at the Garamond Agency. Several themes in the book had their genesis in columns for the *New*

York Times, and for this, I am also grateful to my editors there, Jim Dao and Jamie Reyerson. Jonathan Haidt and Allison Stanger read an early version of the manuscript and gave me valuable comments.

A number of spiritual teachers influenced this book, directly and indirectly. The first is Tenzin Gyatso, His Holiness the Dalai Lama. Our many conversations over the past six years, as well as our writing together, formed large parts of my thinking. Another teacher is Sri Nochur Venkataraman, whom I visited in Palakkad, India, in February 2018. After hours of conversation on the transcendent, he told me that my spiritual guru is my wife, Ester Munt-Brooks. He meant this literally, and I believe this is correct. Through attitude and action, no one in my life has taught me more than she has about love and compassion for all people.

Finally, this book is dedicated to the memory of Father Arne Panula, director of the Catholic Information Center in Washington, DC, until his death in 2017. I began this book in the final weeks of his life. Every month for almost nine years, Father Arne helped me to learn and live the lessons of Matthew 5:44, from which the title is taken.

All royalties from the sale of this book go to support AEI.

Notes

Introduction: Are You Sick of Fighting Yet?

1. Laura Paisley, "Political Polarization at Its Worst since the Civil War," *USC News*, Nov. 8, 2016, https://news.usc .edu/110124/political-polarization-at-its-worst-since-the -civil-war-2.

2. John Whitesides, "From Disputes to a Breakup: Wounds Still Raw after U.S. Election," *Reuters*, Feb. 7, 2017, https://www.reuters.com/article/us-usa-trump -relationships-insight/from-disputes-to-a-breakup -wounds-still-raw-after-u-s-election-idUSKBN15M13L.

3. Justin McCarthy, "Small Majority in U.S. Say the Country's Best Days Are Ahead," Gallup, July 3, 2018, https:// news.gallup.com/poll/236447/small-majority-say-country -best-days-ahead.aspx.

4. "Study: Voters Frustrated That Their Voices Are Not Heard," Congressional Institute, Feb. 3, 2017, https://www.conginst.org/2017/02/03/study-voters-frustrated-that-their-voices-are-not-heard.

5. Chauncey Alcorn, "Speaking at a Trump Rally Made this BLM Activist an Outcast," *VICE*, Oct. 19, 2017, https://www.vice.com/en_us/article/wjx9m4/speaking-at-a-trump-rally-made-this-blm-activist-an-outcast.

6. "Interview with Mother of All Rallies Organizer Tommy Hodges a.k.a. Tommy Gunn," YouTube video, Sept. 16, 2017, https://www.youtube.com/watch?v=9PFhZMvuBHo.

7. Warren D. TenHouten, *Emotion and Reason: Mind, Brain, and the Social Domains of Work and Love* (New York: Routledge, 2013), 18.

8. Arthur Schopenhauer, *The Horrors and Absurdities of Religion: Mankind Is Growing Out of Religion as Out of Its Childhood Clothes*, trans. R. J. Hollingdale (New York: Penguin, 1970), "On Religion: A Dialogue," no. 11.

9. "Contempt," *Encyclopedia of World Problems and Human Potential*, June 17, 2018, http://encyclopedia.uia.org/en/problem/139329.

10. Thomas Aquinas, *Summa Theologica*, I–II, Question 26, Article 4. This is often translated as "To love is to will the good of another."

11. Michael Novak, "Caritas and Economics," *First Things*, July 6, 2009, https://www.firstthings.com/web-exclusives/2009/07/caritas-and-economics.

Chapter 1: The Culture of Contempt

1. Adam Waytz, Liane L. Young, and Jeremy Ginges, "Motive Attribution Asymmetry for Love vs. Hate Drives Intractable Conflict," *Proceedings of the National Academy of Sciences of the United States of America* 111, no. 44 (Nov. 2014): 15687–92, doi: 10.1073/pnas.1414146111.

2. Agneta H. Fischer and Ira J. Roseman, "Beat Them or Ban Them: The Characteristics and Social Functions of Anger and Contempt," *Journal of Personality and Social Psychology* 93, no. 1 (July 2007): 103–15, doi: 10.1037/0022-3514.93.1.103.

3. John M. Gottman, "A Theory of Marital Dissolution and Stability," *Journal of Family Psychology* 7, no. 2 (June 1993): 57–75, doi: 10.1037/0893-3200.7.1.57.

4. Kim T. Buehlman, John M. Gottman, and Lynn F. Katz, "How a Couple Views Their Past Predicts Their Future: Predicting Divorce from an Oral History Interview," *Journal of Family Psychology* 5, nos. 3–4 (Mar.–June 1992): 295–318, doi: 10.1037/0893-3200.5.3-4.295.

5. John M. Gottman, "A Theory of Marital Dissolution and Stability," *Journal of Family Psychology* 7, no. 2 (June 1993): 57–75, doi: 10.1037/0893-3200.7.1.57.

6. Joseph Flaherty, "Arizona Congressman Paul Gosar's Siblings Endorse Rival in New Campaign Ads," *Phoenix New Times*, Sept. 21, 2018, https://www.phoenixnewtimes.com/news/arizona-congressman-paul-gosars-siblings-endorse-opponent-10849863.

7. Paul Gosar (@DrPaulGosar), "My siblings who chose to film ads against me are all liberal Democrats who hate President Trump. These disgruntled Hillary supporters are related by blood to me but like leftists everywhere, they put political ideology before family. Stalin would be proud. #Az04 #MAGA2018," Twitter, Sept. 22, 2018, 11:24 a.m.

8. David A. Graham, "Really, Would You Let Your Daughter Marry a Democrat?" *Atlantic*, Sept. 27, 2012, https://www.theatlantic.com/politics/archive/2012/09/really-would-you-let-your-daughter-marry-a-democrat/262959/.

9. Thomas Jefferson, "From Thomas Jefferson to Henry Lee, 10 August 1824," Rotunda, http://rotunda.upress.virginia.edu/founders/default.xqy?keys=FOEA-print-04-02-02-4451.

10. Agneta H. Fischer and Ira J. Roseman, "Beat Them or Ban Them: The Characteristics and Social Functions of Anger and Contempt."

11. Kirsten Weir, "The Pain of Social Rejection," American Psychological Association, *Monitor on Psychology* 43, no. 4 (Apr. 2012), 50, http://www.apa.org/monitor/2012/04/rejection.aspx.

12. Weir, "Pain of Social Rejection."

13. Stephen Hawkins, et al., "Hidden Tribes: A Study of America's Polarized Landscape," More in Common, 2018, https://static1.squarespace.com/static/5a70a7c3010027736a22740f/t/5bbcea6b7817f7bf7342b718/1539107467397/hidden_tribes_report-2.pdf.

14. John Wagner and Scott Clement, "'It's Just Messed

Up': Most Think Political Divisions as Bad as Vietnam Era, New Poll Shows," *Washington Post*, Oct. 28, 2017, https://www.washingtonpost.com/graphics/2017/national /democracy-poll/?utm_term=.c6b95de49f42.

15. "APA Stress in America Survey: US at 'Lowest Point We Can Remember'; Future of Nation Most Commonly Reported Source of Stress," American Psychological Association, Nov. 1, 2017, http://www.apa.org/news/press /releases/2017/11/lowest-point.aspx.

16. "APA Stress in America Survey."

17. "Many See Potential Harm from Future Gridlock, for the Nation and Personally," Pew Research Center, Dec. 11, 2014, http://www.people-press.org/2014/12/11/few -see-quick-cure-for-nations-political-divisions/12-11 -2014_02.

18. Joshua Bleiberg and Darrell M. West, "Political Polarization on Facebook," May 13, 2015, https://www.brookings .edu/blog/techtank/2015/05/13/political-polarization-on -facebook.

19. Itai Himelboim, Stephen McCreery, and Marc Smith, "Birds of a Feather Tweet Together: Integrating Network and Content Analysis to Examine Cross-Ideology Exposure on Twitter," *Journal of Computer-Mediated Communication* 18, no. 2 (Jan. 2013): 40–60, doi: 10.1111/jcc4.12001.

20. Neil Malhotra and Gregory Huber, "Dimensions of Political Homophily: Isolating Choice Homophily along Political Characteristics," Stanford Graduate School of Business Working Paper No. 3108 (Oct. 2013), https://

www.gsb.stanford.edu/faculty-research/working-papers /dimensions-political-homophily-isolating-choice -homophily-along.

21. "Partisan Animosity, Personal Politics, Views of Trump," Pew Research Center, Oct. 5, 2017, http://www.people -press.org/2017/10/05/8-partisan-animosity-personal -politics-views-of-trump.

22. "Partisan Animosity."

23. "Partisanship and Political Animosity in 2016," Pew Research Center, June 22, 2016, http://www.people-press .org/2016/06/22/partisanship-and-political-animosity-in -2016.

24. David Blankenhorn, "The Top 14 Causes of Political Polarization," *American Interest*, May 16, 2018, https:// www.the-american-interest.com/2018/05/16/the-top-14 -causes-of-political-polarization.

25. "Reelection Rates over the Years," Open Secrets, Center for Responsive Politics, https://www.opensecrets.org /overview/reelect.php. Election results are for 2012, 2014, and 2016; at the time of writing, final results for the 2018 midterms are not available, but the incumbent reelection rate will likely be similar to recent reelection rates of at least 90 percent.

26. Matthew D. Lieberman, *Social: Why Our Brains Are Wired to Connect* (New York: Crown, 2013), 247.

27. Lieberman, *Social*, 247.

28. Julianne Holt-Lunstad, Timothy B. Smith, and J. Bradley Layton, "Social Relationships and Mortality Risk: A Meta

-analytic Review," *PLOS Medicine* 7, no. 7 (July 2010): doi: 10.1371/journal.pmed.1000316.

29. "The Health Benefits of Strong Relationships," *Harvard Women's Health Watch*, Dec. 2010, https://www.health.harvard.edu/newsletter_article/the-health-benefits-of-strong-relationships.

30. "Emory Brain Imaging Studies Reveal Biological Basis for Human Cooperation," Emory Health Sciences Press Release, July 19, 2002, http://whsc.emory.edu/_releases/2002july/altruism.html.

31. "Emory Brain Imaging Studies Reveal Biological Basis for Human Cooperation," Emory Health Sciences Press Release, July 19, 2002, http://whsc.emory.edu/_releases/2002july/altruism.html.

32. Matthew D. Lieberman, *Social: Why Our Brains Are Wired to Connect* (New York: Crown Publishers, 2013).

33. Plato, *The Republic*, trans. Benjamin Jowett (Los Angeles: Madison Park, 2010), 75.

34. Aristotle, *Nicomachean Ethics*, trans. W. D. Ross (Stilwell: Digireads.com, 2005), 8.1.

35. Psalms 133:1 (New International Version).

36. Matthew 12:25 (New International Version).

37. Bhagavad Gita, trans. Stephen Mitchell (New York: Harmony Books, 2000), 186.

38. Thomas Paine, *Common Sense*, Project Gutenberg, June 9, 2008, https://www.gutenberg.org/files/147/147-h/147-h.htm.

39. James Madison, *The Federalist Papers*, No. 14, Avalon

Project, Lillian Goldman Law Library, Yale University, 2008, http://avalon.law.yale.edu/18th_century/fed14.asp.

40. John Adams, "From John Adams to Jonathan Jackson, 2 October 1780," Founders Online, National Archives, last modified June 13, 2018, https://founders.archives.gov /documents/Adams/06-10-02-0113.

41. George Washington, "Washington's Farewell Address," Avalon Project, Lillian Goldman Law Library, Yale University, 2008, http://avalon.law.yale.edu/18th_century /washing.asp.

42. Mark 10: 46–51 (New International Version).

43. "Brief Biography," Office of His Holiness the Dalai Lama, https://www.dalailama.com/the-dalai-lama/biography -and-daily-life/brief-biography.

44. Pico Iyer, *The Open Road: The Global Journey of the Fourteenth Dalai Lama* (New York: Borzoi Books, 2008).

45. Eknath Easwaran, *Essence of the Dhammapada: The Buddha's Call to Nirvana* (Tomales, CA: Nilgiri Press: 2013), 263.

Chapter 2: Can You Afford to Be Nice?

1. Geoffrey C. Urbaniak and Peter R. Kilmann, "Physical Attractiveness and the 'Nice Guy Paradox': Do Nice Guys Really Finish Last?" *Sex Roles* 49, nos. 9–10 (Nov. 2003), doi: 10.1023/A:1025894203368.

2. Edward S. Herold and Robin R. Milhausen, "Dating Preferences of University Women: An Analysis of the

Nice Guy Stereotype," *Journal of Sex & Marital Therapy* 25, no. 4 (Oct.–Dec. 1999): 333–43, doi: 10.1080 /00926239908404010.

3. Wendy Iredale and Mark Van Vugt, "The Peacock's Tail of Altruism," *The Psychologist* 22 (Nov. 2009), https://thepsychologist.bps.org.uk/volume-22/edition-11 /peacocks-tail-altruism.

4. Daniel Farrelly, Paul Clemson, and Melissa Guthrie, "Are Women's Mate Preferences for Altruism Also Influenced by Physical Attractiveness?" *Evolutionary Psychology* 14, no. 1 (Jan.–Mar. 2016): 1–6, doi: 10.1177 /1474704915623698.

5. Gurit E. Birnbaum, et al., "Why Do Men Prefer Nice Women? Gender Typicality Mediates the Effect of Responsiveness on Perceived Attractiveness in Initial Acquaintanceships," *Personality and Social Psychology Bulletin* 40, no. 10 (July 2014): 1341–53, doi: 10.1177 /0146167214543879.

6. Christine L. Porath, Alexandra Gerbasi, and Sebastian L. Schorch, "The Effects of Civility on Advice, Leadership, and Performance," *Journal of Applied Psychology* 100, no. 5 (Sept. 2015): 1527–41, doi: 10.1037/apl0000016.

7. Andrew E. White, Douglas T. Kenrick, and Steven L. Neuberg, "Beauty at the Ballot Box: Disease Threats Predict Preferences for Physically Attractive Leaders," *Psychological Science* 24, no. 12 (Oct. 2013): 2429–36, doi: 10.1177/0956797613493642.

8. Amy J. C. Cuddy, Matthew Kohut, and John Neffinger,

"Connect, Then Lead," *Harvard Business Review*, July–Aug. 2013, https://hbr.org/2013/07/connect-then-lead.

9. James M. Citrin and Richard A. Smith, *The 5 Patterns of Extraordinary Careers* (New York: Crown Business, 2003).

10. Mike Wooldridge, "Mandela Death: How He Survived 27 Years in Prison," BBC News, Dec. 11, 2013, http://www.bbc.com/news/world-africa-23618727.

11. Tal Ben-Shahar, *Choose the Life You Want: The Mindful Way to Happiness* (New York: The Experiment, 2012), 116.

12. James Douglas Laird, "Self-Attribution of Emotion: The Effects of Expressive Behavior on the Quality of Emotional Experience," *Journal of Personality and Social Psychology* 29, no. 4 (May 1974): 475–86, doi: 10.1037/h0036125.

13. Tiffany A. Ito, et al., "The Influence of Facial Feedback on Race Bias," *Psychological Science* 17, no. 3 (Mar. 2006): 256–61, doi: 10.1111/j.1467-9280.2006.01694.x.

14. Paul Ekman and Richard J. Davidson, "Voluntary Smiling Changes Regional Brain Activity," *Psychological Science* 4, no. 5 (Sept. 1993): 342–45, doi: 10.1111/j.1467-9280.1993.tb00576.x.

15. Stephen Covey, *The 7 Habits of Highly Effective People* (New York: Free Press, 1989), 78–80.

16. Arthur Aron, Edward Melinat, and Elaine N. Aron, "The Experimental Generation of Interpersonal Closeness: A Procedure and Some Preliminary Findings," *Personality and Social Psychology Bulletin* 23, no. 4 (Apr. 1997): 363–77, doi: 10.1177/0146167297234003.

17. Mandy Len Catron, "To Fall in Love with Anyone, Do This," *New York Times*, Jan. 9, 2015, https://www.nytimes.com/2015/01/11/fashion/modern-love-to-fall-in-love-with-anyone-do-this.html.

18. Randee Dawn and Melissa Dunlop, "36 Questions to Reignite the Flame: Love Quiz by Arthur Aron," *Today*, Feb. 17, 2015, https://www.today.com/health/36-questions-reignite-flame-love-quiz-couples-t3221.

19. Dale Carnegie, *How to Win Friends & Influence People* (New York: Pocket Books, 1936), 53–54.

20. Robert A. Emmons and Michael E. McCullough, "Counting Blessings versus Burdens: An Experimental Investigation of Gratitude and Subjective Well-Being in Daily Life," *Journal of Personality and Social Psychology* 84, no. 2 (Feb. 2003): 377–89, doi: 10.1037/0022-3514.84.2.377.

21. Luke 6: 32, 35 (New International Version).

22. Abraham Lincoln, "First Inaugural Address of Abraham Lincoln," Avalon Project, Lillian Goldman Law Library, Yale University, 2008, http://avalon.law.yale.edu/19th_century/lincoln1.asp.

Chapter 3: Love Lessons for Leaders

1. Daniel Kahneman, et al., "A Survey Method for Characterizing Daily Life Experience: The Day Reconstruction Method," *Science* 306, no. 5702 (Dec. 3, 2004): 1776–80, doi: 10.1126/science.1103572.

2. Niccolò Machiavelli, *The Prince*, trans. Harvey C. Mansfield (Chicago: University of Chicago Press, 1985), 66.

3. Daniel Goleman, "Leadership That Gets Results," *Harvard Business Review*, Mar.–Apr. 2000, https://hbr.org/2000/03/leadership-that-gets-results.

4. Martin Luther King Jr., "MLK Quote of the Week," King Center, Apr. 9, 2013, http://www.thekingcenter.org/blog/mlk-quote-week-all-labor-uplifts-humanity-has-dignity-and-importance-and-should-be-undertaken.

5. Nicholas Eberstadt, "Men Without Work," *American Consequences*, Jan. 30, 2018, https://americanconsequences.com/men-without-work.

6. Eberstadt, "Men Without Work."

7. Eberstadt, "Men Without Work."

8. Anne Case and Angus Deaton, "Rising Morbidity and Mortality in Midlife among White Non-Hispanic Americans in the 21st Century," *Proceedings of the National Academy of Sciences of the United States of America* 112, no. 49 (Dec. 8, 2015): 15078–83, doi: 10.1073/pnas.1518393112.

9. "Overdose Death Rates," National Institute on Drug Abuse, Aug. 2018, https://www.drugabuse.gov/related-topics/trends-statistics/overdose-death-rates.

10. Sally Satel, "Taking on the Scourge of Opioids," *National Affairs* 37 (Summer 2017): 3–21, https://www.nationalaffairs.com/publications/detail/taking-on-the-scourge-of-opioids.

11. "Working-Class Whites Poll," Kaiser Family Foundation/CNN, Sept. 21, 2016, http://files.kff.org/attachment

/Kaiser-Family-Foundation-CNN-Working-Class
-Whites-Poll-Topline-Day-3.

12. Danielle Kurtzleben, "Here's How Many Bernie Sanders Supporters Ultimately Voted for Trump," NPR, Aug. 24, 2017, https://www.npr.org/2017/08/24/545812242/1-in -10-sanders-primary-voters-ended-up-supporting-trump -survey-finds.

13. Jeff Stein, "The Bernie Voters Who Defected to Trump, Explained by a Political Scientist," *Vox*, Aug. 24, 2017, https://www.vox.com/policy-and-politics/2017/8/24 /16194086/bernie-trump-voters-study.

14. "Exit Polls," CNN, Nov. 23, 2016, https://www.cnn.com /election/2016/results/exit-polls.

15. Matthew Yglesias, "What Really Happened in 2016," *Vox*, Sept. 18, 2017, https://www.vox.com/policy-and-politics /2017/9/18/16305486/what-really-happened-in-2016.

16. Shannon Monnat and Scott Simon, "Study: Communities Most Affected by Opioid Epidemic Also Voted for Trump," NPR, Dec. 17, 2016, https://www.npr.org/2016 /12/17/505965420/study-communities-most-affected-by -opioid-epidemic-also-voted-for-trump.

17. Philip Bump, "The Counties That Flipped Parties to Swing the 2016 Election," *Washington Post*, Nov. 15, 2016, https://www.washingtonpost.com/news/the-fix/wp/2016 /11/15/the-counties-that-flipped-parties-to-swing-the -2016-election/?utm_term=.a7008c8b78cb.

18. Paul O'Connell, Debra Pepler, and Wendy Craig, "Peer Involvement in Bullying: Insights and Challenges for

Intervention," *Journal of Adolescence* 22, no. 2 (Aug. 1999): 437–52, doi: 10.1006/jado.1999.0238.

19. Jean Lipman-Blumen, *The Allure of Toxic Leaders: Why We Follow Destructive Bosses and Corrupt Politicians—and How We Can Survive Them* (Oxford: Oxford University Press, 2005).

20. Jennifer S. Lerner and Larissa Z. Tiedens, "Portrait of the Angry Decision Maker: How Appraisal Tendencies Shape Anger's Influence on Cognition," *Journal of Behavioral Decision Making* 19, no. 2 (Apr. 2006): 115–37, doi: doi .org/10.1002/bdm.515.

21. Matthew 10:34 (New International Version).

22. James Q. Wilson, *The Moral Sense* (New York: Free Press, 1993), 246.

23. "This Is What Happened When Black Lives Matter Activists Were Invited on Stage at a Pro-Trump Rally," NowThis Politics, Sept. 18, 2017, https://www.facebook .com/NowThisPolitics/videos/1912736818757799. At the time of this writing (Oct. 12, 2018), this video has fifty -seven million views.

24. Jeffrey M. Jones, "Americans Divided on Whether King's Dream Has Been Realized," Gallup, Aug. 26, 2011, http:// news.gallup.com/poll/149201/americans-divided-whether -king-dream-realized.aspx.

Chapter 4: How Can I Love My Enemies If They Are Immoral?

1. David Brooks, "If It Feels Right . . . ," *New York Times*, Sept. 12, 2011, https://www.nytimes.com/2011/09/13/opinion/if-it-feels-right.html.

2. Jonathan Haidt and Jesse Graham, "When Morality Opposes Justice: Conservatives Have Moral Intuitions that Liberals May Not Recognize," *Social Justice Research* 20, no. 1 (Mar. 2007): 98–116, doi: 10.1007/s11211-007-0034-z; and Jesse Graham, Jonathan Haidt, and Brian A. Nosek, "Liberals and Conservatives Rely on Different Sets of Moral Foundations," *Journal of Personality and Social Psychology* 96, no. 5 (May 2009): 1029–46, doi: 10.1037/a0015141.

3. Augustine, *The Confessions*, trans. Maria Boulding (New York: New City Press, 1997), 9.

4. Ben Kenward and Matilda Dahl, "Preschoolers Distribute Scarce Resources According to the Moral Valence of Recipients' Previous Actions," *Developmental Psychology* 47, no. 4 (July 2011): 1054–64, doi: 10.1037/a0023869.

5. Rimma Teper, Michael Inzlicht, and Elizabeth Page-Gould, "Are We More Moral than We Think? The Role of Affect in Moral Behavior and Moral Forecasting," *Psychological Science* 22, no. 4 (Mar. 2011): 553–58, doi: 10.1177/0956797611402513.

6. F. A. Hayek, *The Road to Serfdom: Text and Documents—*

The Definitive Edition, ed. Bruce Caldwell (Chicago: The University of Chicago Press, 2007), 148.

7. Ronald Reagan, *First Inaugural Address*, Jan. 5, 1967, http://governors.library.ca.gov/addresses/33-Reagan01 .html.

8. Jennifer Epstein, "Obama Tells Kids to Study, Not Watch 'Real Housewives,'" *Politico*, July 25, 2012, https://www .politico.com/blogs/politico44/2012/07/obama-tells-kids -to-study-not-watch-real-housewives-130139.

9. Scott Clement, "Hard-Working Taxpayers Don't Support Big Cuts to Food Stamps, It Turns Out," *Washington Post*, May 25, 2017, https://www.washingtonpost.com/news /the-fix/wp/2017/05/25/hard-working-taxpayers-dont -support-big-cuts-to-food-stamps-it-turns-out/?utm _term=.fc5543d3ad29.

10. "Poll: Voters Want Welfare Reform," Foundation for Government Accountability, Feb. 1, 2018, https://thefga .org/poll/poll-voters-want-welfare-reform.

11. Barton Gellman, "Turning an About-Face into a Forward March," *Washington Post*, Apr. 1, 1993, https://www .washingtonpost.com/archive/politics/1993/04/01/turning -an-about-face-into-a-forward-march/3be67522-209e -4849-a738-c60e9fadbb1a/?utm_term=.996823164eff.

12. David Wright and Sunlen Miller, "Obama Dropped Flag Pin in War Statement," ABC News, Oct. 4, 2007, https:// abcnews.go.com/Politics/story?id=3690000&page=1.

13. Angie Drobnic Holan, "Obama Contradicts Previously Stated Pin Philosophy," *Politifact*, Apr. 18, 2008, https://

www.politifact.com/truth-o-meter/statements/2008/apr/18/barack-obama/obama-contradicts-previously-stated-pin-philosophy/.

14. "National Public Opinion Survey, 2017," Remington Research Group, Sept. 25, 2017, http://remingtonrg.wpengine.com/wp-content/uploads/2017/03/NFL_9-25-17.pdf.

15. "Sex and Unexpected Pregnancies: What Evangelical Millennials Think and Practice," Grey Matter Research for National Association of Evangelicals, May 2012, https://www.nae.net/sex-and-unexpected-pregnancies.

16. George H. Gallup Jr., "Current Views on Premarital, Extramarital Sex," Gallup, June 24, 2003, http://news.gallup.com/poll/8704/current-views-premarital-extramarital-sex.aspx.

17. Jonathan Haidt, Evan Rosenberg, and Holly Hom, "Differentiating Diversities: Moral Diversity Is Not Like Other Kinds," *Journal of Applied Social Pyschology* 33, no. 1 (Jan. 2003): 1–36, doi:10.1111/j.1559-1816.2003.tb02071.x.

18. Shanto Iyengar, Tobias Konitzer, and Kent Tedin, "The Home as a Political Fortress: Family Agreement in an Era of Polarization," *Journal of Politics* 80, no. 4 (Oct. 2018): 1326–38, doi: 10.1086/698929.

19. Shanto Iyengar and Sean J. Westwood, "Fear and Loathing across Party Lines: New Evidence on Group Polarization," *American Journal of Political Science* 59, no. 3 (July 2015): 690–707, doi:10.1111/ajps.12152.

20. Gary Marcus, *The Birth of the Mind: How a Tiny Number of Genes Creates the Complexities of Human Thought* (New York: Basic Books, 2004), 34–40.

21. Luke 18: 11–13 (New International Version).

Chapter 5: The Power and Peril of Identity

1. Richard T. LaPiere, "Attitudes vs. Actions," *Social Forces* 13, no. 2 (Dec. 1934): 230–37, doi: 10.2307/2570339.

2. See, for example: Thomas C. Schelling, "Dynamic Models of Segregation," *Journal of Mathematical Sociology* 1, no. 2 (1971): 143–86, doi: 10.1080/0022250X.1971.9989794.

3. Robert D. Putnam, *Bowling Alone: The Collapse and Revival of American Community* (New York: Simon & Schuster Paperbacks, 2000), 19.

4. Putnam, *Bowling Alone*, 22.

5. Putnam, *Bowling Alone*, 23.

6. Natalie J. Grove and Anthony B. Zwi, "Our Health and Theirs: Forced Migration, Othering, and Public Health," *Social Science & Medicine* 62, no. 8 (Apr. 2006): 1931–42, doi: 10.1016/j.socscimed.2005.08.061.

7. Robert D. Putnam, "*E Pluribus Unum*: Diversity and Community in the Twenty-First Century," *Scandinavian Political Studies* 30, no. 2 (June 2007): 137–74, doi: 10.1111/j.1467-9477.2007.00176.x.

8. Putnam, "*E Pluribus Unum*."

9. Gregory Boyle, *Tattoos on the Heart: The Power of Boundless Compassion* (New York: Free Press, 2010), 6–8.

Chapter 6: Tell Me a Story

1. John Adams, "Adams' Argument for the Defense: 3–4 December 1770," Founders Online, National Archives, last modified June 13, 2018, https://founders.archives.gov /documents/Adams/05-03-02-0001-0004-0016.

2. Thorstein Veblen, "Why Is Economics Not an Evolutionary Science?" *Quarterly Journal of Economics* 12, no. 4 (July 1898): 373–97.

3. Elizabeth Kolbert, "That's What You Think," *New Yorker*, Feb. 27, 2017, online as "Why Facts Don't Change Our Minds," https://www.newyorker.com/magazine/2017 /02/27/why-facts-dont-change-our-minds.

4. Uri Hasson, "This Is Your Brain on Communication," TED Talk video, Feb. 2016, https://www.ted.com/talks /uri_hasson_this_is_your_brain_on_communication /transcript.

5. Uri Hasson, "Defend Your Research: I Can Make Your Brain Look Like Mine," *Harvard Business Review*, Dec. 2010, https://hbr.org/2010/12/defend-your-research-i-can -make-your-brain-look-like-mine.

6. Uri Hasson, et al., "Brain-to-Brain Coupling: A Mechanism for Creating and Sharing a Social World," *Trends in Cognitive Sciences* 16, no. 2: 114–21, doi:10.1016 /j.tics.2011.12.007.

7. "Big Ben Bowen (St. Jude Children's Research Hospital)," YouTube video, July 26, 2008, https://www.youtube.com /watch?v=XxEHlyF3sV0.

8. Paul J. Zak, "Trust, Morality—and Oxytocin?" TED Talk video, July 2011, https://www.ted.com/talks/paul_zak _trust_morality_and_oxytocin/transcript?language=en.

9. Paul J. Zak, "How Stories Change the Brain," *Greater Good Magazine*, Dec. 17, 2013, https://greatergood.berkeley .edu/article/item/how_stories_change_brain.

10. Pei-Ying Lin, et al., "Oxytocin Increases the Influence of Public Service Advertisements," *PLOS ONE* 8, no. 2 (Feb. 2013): 1–10, doi: 10.1371/journal.pone.0056934.

11. "UNICEF Urges Swift Action, 'Robust Financing' to Close Water and Sanitation Gaps in Sub-Saharan Africa," *UN News*, Dec. 16, 2015, https://www.un.org/sustainable development/blog/2015/12/unicef-urges-swift-action-robust -financing-to-close-water-and-sanitation-gaps-in-sub -saharan-africa.

12. Parul Sehgal, "Fighting 'Erasure,'" *New York Times Magazine*, Feb. 2, 2016, https://www.nytimes.com/2016/02/07 /magazine/the-painful-consequences-of-erasure.html.

13. Anton Antonov-Ovseyenko, *The Time of Stalin: Portrait of a Tyranny* (Harper & Row, 1981), 278.

14. Norman M. Naimark, *Stalin's Genocides* (Princeton, NJ: Princeton University Press, 2010), 59.

15. *Der Ewige Jude* [The Eternal Jew], United States Holocaust Memorial Museum, https://encyclopedia.ushmm.org /content/en/article/der-ewige-jude.

16. Kennedy Ndahiro, "Dehumanisation: How Tutsis Were Reduced to Cockroaches, Snakes to Be Killed," *New*

Times, Mar. 13, 2014, http://www.newtimes.co.rw/section/read/73836.

17. Gustave Le Bon, *The Crowd: A Study of the Popular Mind* (London: T. Fisher Unwin, 1896).

18. "Gustave Le Bon," *Encyclopaedia Britannica*, https://www.britannica.com/biography/Gustave-Le-Bon#ref246264.

19. Edward Diener, et al., "Effects of Deindividuation Variables on Stealing among Halloween Trick-or-Treaters," *Journal of Personality and Social Psychology* 33, no. 2 (Feb. 1976): 178–83, doi:10.1037/0022-3514.33.2.178.

20. Chen-Bo Zhong, Vanessa K. Bohns, and Francesca Gino, "Good Lamps Are the Best Police: Darkness Increases Dishonesty and Self-Interested Behavior," *Psychological Science* 21, no. 3 (Mar. 2010): 311–14, doi: 10.1177/0956797609360754.

21. John 3:20–21 (New International Version).

22. Erin E. Buckels, Paul D. Trapnell, and Delroy L. Paulhus, "Trolls Just Want to Have Fun," *Personality and Individual Differences* 67 (Feb. 2014): 97–102, doi:10.1016/j.paid.2014.01.016.

23. Melissa G. Hunt, et al., "No More FOMO: Limiting Social Media Decreases Loneliness and Depression," *Journal of Social and Clinical Psychology* 37, no. 10 (Dec. 2018): 751–68, doi: 10.1521/jscp.2018.37.10.751.

24. Carol Glatz, "Pope Francis: Priests Should Be 'Shepherds Living with the Smell of the Sheep,'" *Catholic Telegraph*,

March 28, 2013, https://www.thecatholictelegraph.com/pope-francis-priests-should-be-shepherds-living-with-the-smell-of-the-sheep/13439.

Chapter 7: Is Competition Our Problem?

1. Michael Ryan, "School Board Axes Dodgeball Games from Curriculum," *Windham Patch*, Mar. 21, 2013, https://patch.com/new-hampshire/windham/school-board-axes-dodgeball-games-from-curriculum.
2. Ryan, "School Board Axes Dodgeball."
3. Neil F. Williams, "The Physical Education Hall of Shame," *Journal of Physical Education, Recreation & Dance* 63, no. 6 (Aug. 1992): 57–60, doi:10.1080/07303084.1992.10606620.
4. Jiddu Krishnamurti, *Krishnamurti on Education* (Ojai: Krishnamurti Foundation, 1974), 106.
5. Cindy Wooden, "Communion, Not Competition, Is Key to Job Growth, Pope Says," *Crux*, Oct. 26, 2017, https://cruxnow.com/vatican/2017/10/26/communion-not-competition-key-job-growth-pope-says.
6. Allan Dowd, "Women's Ice Hockey Game Must Improve, Says Rogge," Reuters, Feb. 25, 2010, https://www.reuters.com/article/idINIndia-46488520100226.
7. Rebecca R. Ruiz, "Mystery in Sochi Doping Case Lies with Tamper-Proof Bottle," *New York Times*, May 13, 2016, https://www.nytimes.com/2016/05/14/sports/russia-doping-bottles-olympics-2014.html.

8. Kristin Toussaint, "Newspaper Headlines on Tom Brady's Deflategate Suspension," Boston.com, May 12, 2015, https://www.boston.com/sports/new-england-patriots/2015/05/12/newspaper-headlines-on-tom-bradys-deflategate-suspension.

9. "Deflategate Newspaper Headlines," *Sports Illustrated*, Jan. 23, 2015, https://www.si.com/nfl/photos/2015/01/23/deflategate-tom-brady-new-england-patriots-headlines#4.

10. Rick Chandler, "Robert Kraft Crashes Belichick Super Bowl Press Conference to Rant about DeflateGate," *SportsGrid*, Jan. 26, 2015, https://www.sportsgrid.com/real-sports/nfl/robert-kraft-crashes-belichick-super-bowl-press-conference-to-rant-about-deflategate.

11. "Wendy's Commercial—Soviet Fashion Show," YouTube video, Sept. 3, 2006, https://www.youtube.com/watch?v=5CaMUfxVJVQ.

12. Maxim Pinkovskiy and Xavier Sala-i-Martin, "Parametric Estimations of the World Distribution of Income," National Bureau of Economic Research, NBER Working Paper No. 15433 (Oct. 2009), doi: 10.3386/w15433.

13. Barack Obama in "Remarks by the President in Conversation on Poverty at Georgetown University," Office of the Press Secretary, May 12, 2015, https://obamawhitehouse.archives.gov/the-press-office/2015/05/12/remarks-president-conversation-poverty-georgetown-university.

14. Philip Elmer-DeWitt, "Transcript: Apple CEO Tim Cook

at Goldman Sachs," *Fortune*, Feb. 15, 2012, http://fortune
.com/2012/02/15/transcript-apple-ceo-tim-cook-at
-goldman-sachs.

15. Courtney Eldridge, "A More Perfect Union," *New York Times Magazine*, June 18, 2000, http://movies2.nytimes
.com/library/magazine/home/20000618mag-shoptalk.html.

16. Bruce Drake, "Americans See Growing Gap between Rich and Poor," Pew Research Center, Dec. 5, 2013, http://
www.pewresearch.org/fact-tank/2013/12/05/americans
-see-growing-gap-between-rich-and-poor.

17. "Americans Stand Out on Individualism," Pew Research Center, Oct. 7, 2014, http://www.pewglobal.org/2014/10
/09/emerging-and-developing-economies-much-more
-optimistic-than-rich-countries-about-the-future/pg_14
-09-04_usindividualism_640-px.

18. Alexis de Tocqueville, *Democracy in America*, trans. Harvey C. Mansfield and Delba Winthrop (Chicago: University of Chicago Press, 2000), 187–89.

19. De Tocqueville, *Democracy in America*, 187–89.

20. John Stuart Mill, *Principles of Political Economy* (London: Longmans, Green, and Co., 1911), 351–52.

21. Maria L. La Ganga, "Clinton Slams Trump's 'Racist Ideology' That Ushers Hate Groups into Mainstream," *Guardian*, Aug. 25, 2016, https://www.theguardian.com
/us-news/2016/aug/25/hillary-clinton-alt-right-racism
-speech-donald-trump-nevada; and Donald Trump (@realDonaldTrump): "Crooked Hillary Clinton is the worst (and biggest) loser of all time. She just can't stop,

which is so good for the Republican Party. Hillary, get on with your life and give it another try in three years!," Twitter, Nov. 18, 2017, 5:31 a.m.

22. Proverbs 27:17 (New International Version).

23. Edmund Burke, *Maxims and Opinions, Moral, Political and Economical, with Characters, from the Works of the Right Hon. Edmund Burke*, vol. 1 (London: C. Whittingham, 1804), 79.

24. Vincent Price, Joseph N. Cappella, and Lilach Nir, "Does Disagreement Contribute to More Deliberative Opinion?" *Political Communication* 19, no. 1 (Jan. 2002): 95–112, doi: 10.1080/105846002317246506.

25. Xueming Luo, Vamsi K. Kanuri, and Michelle Andrews, "How Does CEO Tenure Matter? The Mediating Role of Firm-Employee and Firm-Customer Relationships, *Strategic Management Journal* 35, no. 4 (Apr. 2014): doi:10.1002/smj.2112.

26. John Baldoni, "Hire People Who Disagree with You," *Harvard Business Review*, July 27, 2009, https://hbr.org/2009/07/hire-people-who-disagree.

27. Katherine W. Phillips, Katie A. Liljenquist, Margaret A. Neale, "Is the Pain Worth the Gain? The Advantages and Liabilities of Agreeing with Socially Distinct Newcomers," *Personality and Social Psychology Bulletin* 35, no. 3 (Mar. 2009): 336–50, doi: 10.1177/0146167208328062.

28. José L. Duarte, et al., "Political Diversity Will Improve Social Psychological Science," *Behavioral and Brain Sciences* 38, July 18, 2014, e130, doi: 10.1017/S0140525X14000430.

29. Yoel Inbar and Joris Lammers, "Political Diversity in Social and Personality Psychology," *Perspectives on Psychological and Personality Psychology* 7, no. 5 (Sept. 5, 2012): 496–503, doi: 10.1177/1745691612448792.

30. John Adams, "Thoughts on Government," Apr. 1776, *Papers of John Adams*, ed. Robert J. Taylor, et al. (Cambridge, MA: Belknap Press of Harvard University Press, 1977), vol. 4, pp. 86–93, in *The Founders' Constitution*, ed. Philip B. Kurland (Chicago: University of Chicago Press, 1987), vol. 1, ch. 4, doc. 5, http://press-pubs.uchicago.edu/founders/documents/v1ch4s5.html.

31. Massachusetts Constitution, article VII, part I.

32. "World Values Survey Wave 6 (2010–2014)," World Values Survey, Apr. 29, 2014, http://www.worldvaluessurvey.org/WVSDocumentationWV6.jsp.

Chapter 8: Please Disagree with Me

1. Robert George, Timothy George, and Chuck Colson, "Manhattan Declaration: A Call of Christian Conscience," Nov. 20, 2009, https://www.manhattandeclaration.org/.

2. John Carney, "Cornel West Blasts Obama as a 'Mascot of Wall Street,'" CNBC, May 18, 2011, https://www.cnbc.com/id/43080122.

3. Quotations from Robby George and Cornel West in this chapter are drawn from videos of several public speaking engagements, including: "Cornel West and Robert George '77 Hold Collection on Campus," You-

Tube video, Nov. 7, 2017, https://www.youtube.com /watch?v=H6m4C_YOKUo&t=737s; "Cornel West and Robert George: The Examined Life | Live Stream," You-Tube video, Nov. 30, 2016, https://www.youtube.com /watch?v=SER_TruGo2o&t=887s; "Hauenstein Cen-ter American Conversations: Robert P. George and Cor-nel West," YouTube video, Apr. 10, 2015, https://www .youtube.com/watch?v=M7pCmGna_20&t=670s; and "AEI Annual Dinner 2016: A Conversation with Ir-ving Kristol Honoree Robby George," YouTube video, Sep. 28, 2016, https://www.youtube.com/watch?v=-Ksk RUhSc4U.

4. Quotations of Aristotle in this chapter are taken from the *Nichomachean Ethics*, Book 8, parts 3 and 11, and Book 9, part 6, translated by W. D. Ross and posted on the web-site of the Massachusetts Institute of Technology, http:// classics.mit.edu/Aristotle/nicomachaen.8.viii.html and http://classics.mit.edu/Aristotle/nicomachaen.9.ix.html.

5. Emily J. Brontë, "Love and Friendship" in *The Complete Poems of Emily Jane Brontë*, ed. C. W. Hatfield (New York: Columbia University Press, 1941), 130–31.

6. Fulton J. Sheen, *Three to Get Married* (Princeton, NJ: Scepter Publishers, 1951).

7. Robert P. George and Cornel West, "Truth Seeking, De-mocracy, and Freedom of Thought and Expression," James Madison Program in American Ideals and Institu-tions, Princeton University, Mar. 14, 2017, https://jmp .princeton.edu/statement.

8. Danny Westneat, "In Seattle, Is It Now Taboo to Be Friends with a Republican?" *Seattle Times*, June 2, 2017, https://www.seattletimes.com/seattle-news/politics/in -seattle-is-it-now-taboo-to-be-friends-with-a-republican.

9. Dale Carnegie, *How to Win Friends and Influence People* (New York: Pocket Books, 1936), 110–11.

10. Aaron Blake, "Hillary Clinton Takes Her 'Deplorables' Argument for Another Spin," *Washington Post*, Mar. 13, 2018, https://www.washingtonpost.com/news/the-fix /wp/2018/03/12/hillary-clinton-takes-her-deplorables -argument-for-another-spin/?utm_term=.45639cef38e4.

11. Robert P. Abelson and James C. Miller, "Negative Persuasion via Personal Insult," *Journal of Experimental Social Psychology* 3, no. 4 (Oct. 1967): 321–33.

12. Nielsen Company, "Third Presidential Debate of 2016 Draws 71.6 Million Viewers," Oct. 20, 2016, http://www .nielsen.com/us/en/insights/news/2016/third-presidential -debate-of-2016-draws-71-6-million-viewers.html.

13. Douglas J. Ahler and Gaurav Sood, "The Parties in Our Heads: Misperceptions about Party Composition and Their Consequences," *Journal of Politics* 80, no. 3 (Apr. 2018): doi: 10.1086/697253.

14. Kim Parker, et al., "What Unites and Divides Urban, Suburban and Rural Communities," Pew Research Center (May 2018), http://www.pewsocialtrends.org/2018/05 /22/what-unites-and-divides-urban-suburban-and-rural -communities.

15. Jacqueline Thomsen, "GOP Pa. Candidate: 'The Other

Side' Has 'Hatred' for Trump, Country, and God," *The Hill*, Mar. 12, 2018, https://thehill.com/homenews/campaign/378059-gop-candidate-the-other-side-has-hatred-for-president-country-and-god.

16. Ronald Reagan, "Labor Day Speech at Liberty State Park, Jersey City, New Jersey," Ronald Reagan Presidential Library and Museum, Sep. 1, 1980, https://www.reaganlibrary.gov/9-1-80.

Conclusion: Five Rules to Subvert the Culture of Contempt

1. Margaret Wise Brown, *The Important Book* (New York: Harper and Brothers, 1949).

2. Dalai Lama. "I'm Tibetan, I'm Buddhist and I'm the Dalai Lama, but if I emphasize these differences it sets me apart and raises barriers with other people. What we need to do is to pay more attention to the ways in which we are the same as other people," Twitter, May 21, 2018, 2:35 a.m.

About the Author

Arthur C. Brooks is president of the American Enterprise Institute (AEI), where he also holds the Beth and Ravenel Curry Chair in Free Enterprise. He is the author of eleven books, including the bestsellers *The Conservative Heart* and *The Road to Freedom*. He is a columnist for the *Washington Post* and the host of the podcast *The Arthur Brooks Show*. Previously, he spent twelve years as a professional classical musician in the United States and Spain, including several seasons as a member of the City Orchestra of Barcelona. A native of Seattle, Brooks lives with his family in Bethesda, Maryland. In the fall of 2019, he will join the faculty of the Harvard Kennedy School and Harvard Business School.